The Apollo Program: The History and Legacy of America's Most Famous Space Missions

By Charles River Editors

Gus Grissom, Ed White, and Roger Chaffee in front of the launch pad 10 days before the disaster

About Charles River Editors

Charles River Editors provides superior editing and original writing services in the digital publishing industry, with the expertise to create digital content for publishers across a vast range of subject matter. In addition to providing original digital content for third party publishers, we also republish civilization's greatest literary works, bringing them to new generations of readers via ebooks.

Sign up here to receive updates about free books as we publish them, and visit Our Kindle Author Page to browse today's free promotions and our most recently published Kindle titles.

Introduction

The insignia for the Apollo 1 mission

The Apollo Missions

"There's always a possibility that you can have a catastrophic failure, of course; this can happen on any flight; it can happen on the last one as well as the first one. So, you just plan as best you can to take care of all these eventualities, and you get a well-trained crew and you go fly." - Gus Grissom, December 1966

The Apollo space program is the most famous and celebrated in American history, but the first successful landing of men on the Moon during Apollo 11 had complicated roots dating back over a decade, and it also involved one of NASA's most infamous tragedies. Landing on the Moon presented an ideal goal all on its own, but the government's urgency in designing the Apollo program was actually brought about by the Soviet Union, which spent much of the 1950s leaving the United States in its dust (and rocket fuel). In 1957, at a time when people were concerned about communism and nuclear war, many Americans were dismayed by news that the Soviet Union was successfully launching satellites into orbit.

Among those concerned was President Dwight D. Eisenhower, whose space program was clearly lagging a few years behind the Soviets' space program. From 1959-1963, the United States worked toward putting satellites and humans into orbit via the Mercury program, but Eisenhower's administration was already designing plans for the Apollo program by 1960, a year before the first Russian orbited the Earth and two years before John Glenn became the first American to orbit the Earth.

On May 25, 1961, President John F. Kennedy addressed Congress and asked the nation to "commit itself to achieving the goal, before this decade is out, of landing a man on the Moon and returning him safely to the Earth." Given America's inability to even put a man in orbit yet, this seemed like an overly ambitious goal, and it isn't even clear that Kennedy himself believed it possible; after all, he was reluctant to meet NASA Administrator James E. Webb's initial funding requests.

As Apollo 11's name suggests, there were actually a number of Apollo missions that came before, many of which included testing the rockets and different orbital and lunar modules in orbit. In fact, it wasn't until Apollo 8 that a manned vehicle was sent towards the Moon and back, and before that mission, the most famous Apollo mission was Apollo 1, albeit for all the wrong reasons.

There were no delusions regarding the dangers of manned space travel, but they were brought home on January 27, 1967, when all three astronauts were killed by a fire that ignited in the cabin during a launch rehearsal. To this day, there is still debate over what ignited the fire, but the disaster made clear that the modules being used by NASA had a series of fatal flaws. After the Apollo 1 tragedy, NASA changed its plans by first running a series of unmanned missions to test the Saturn rockets and the different modules throughout 1967 and early 1968. and it would not be until Apollo 7 launched about 20 months after the disaster that NASA dared to conduct another manned mission.

At 9:32 a.m. on July 16, 1969, time stood still throughout the world, as thousands converged on the Kennedy Space Center and millions tuned in on live television. At that instant, the first rumbles began to shake the ground, as a small spacecraft attached to the giant Saturn V rocket several hundred feet tall started lifting off. Quickly being propelled several thousand miles per hour, it takes just a few minutes to reach a speed of 15,000 miles per hour, and just a few more minutes to enter orbit at 18,000 miles per hour. Apollo 11 was on its way to a historic first landing on the Moon.

Apollo 11's trip to the Moon may have started on that day in 1969, but the journey had begun over a decade earlier as part of the Space Race between the United States and the Soviet Union. While landing on the Moon was a noble goal proposed as early as 1961 by President Kennedy, NASA and the nation as a whole moved with urgency simply to best the Soviet Union, which had spent the 1950s beating America to important space-related firsts, including launching the first satellite and cosmonaut in orbit. In fact, President Eisenhower's administration began the design for the Apollo program in 1960 in hopes of getting a head start to the Moon, despite the fact the plans originated a year before the first Russian cosmonaut, Yuri Gagarin, orbited the Earth and two years before John Glenn did.

Over the decade, NASA would spend tens of billions on the Apollo missions, the most expensive peacetime program in American history to that point, and even though Apollo 11 was only one of almost 20 Apollo missions, it was certainly the crown jewel. only one of nearly 20 Apollo missions conducted by NASA. And to make Apollo 11 a success, it would take nearly a decade of planning by government officials, hard work by NASA scientists, intense training by the astronauts, and several missions preceding Apollo 11. It also cost over $20 billion, making the Apollo program the most expensive peacetime program in American history at the time.

Americans sure felt the cost was worth it as they watched the first live shots of astronauts Neil Armstrong and Buzz Aldrin walking on the Moon. As he left his first footprint on the Moon, Armstrong transmitted one of the 20th century's most famous phrases: "That's one small step for man, one giant leap for mankind."

Apollo 12 successfully landed astronauts on the Moon just a few months after Apollo 11's successful mission. Apollo 12 was actually more successful than Apollo 11 from the standpoint of fulfilling the mission objectives, but it was naturally overshadowed since it did not come first.

Another reason Apollo 12 is mostly forgotten today can be credited to the dramatic and fateful Apollo 13 mission, which took twists and turns nobody could have predicted when it launched on April 11, 1970. Apollo 13's mission was to land on the Moon near the Fra Mauro highlands, which were hills that had somehow formed in the middle of a huge crater tens of miles wide. The mission was supposed to test for seismic activity and take samples to analyze the crater and try to find an explanation for the formation of the hills.

Of course, as is widely known today, Apollo 13 never made the landing. The ever-dependable Saturn V properly thrust Apollo 13 out of the Earth's orbit and toward the Moon, but two days into the voyage, the crew heard a loud bang. At first, the crew was not sure what had happened, leading Commander James Lovell to famously transmit to Mission Control, "Houston, we've had a problem." As it turned out, one of the main oxygen tanks had ruptured in the Service Module, causing a catastrophic failure. The Command/Service Module's fuel cells all shut down, leaving the command/Service Module to run on backup batteries. In other words, Apollo 13 was adrift between the Earth and the Moon with limited battery power.

With severely limited supplies and power, Apollo 13 shut down the Command/Service Module altogether, and the entire crew had to rely on camping out in the Lunar Module, which was only equipped to support two astronauts. The Moon landing was obviously out of the question, but Apollo 13 still had to orbit around the Moon to head back to Earth, a trip that would take four more days. Power and water were the two most critical shortages, forcing the crew to maintain the Lunar Module at low energy. The crew also had to worry about carbon dioxide building up and poisoning them, because the Lunar Module's system to remove carbon dioxide was designed to support two people for a few days, not three people for four days.

Once Apollo 13 rounded the Moon and headed back to Earth, the crew and Mission Control managed to restart the Command/Service Module, rerouting power from the Lunar Module to the Command/Service Module. The crew also had to manually realign the spacecraft for reentry, as Lovell had done for Apollo 8. Before reentry, the Service Module was jettisoned from the spacecraft, and pictures of it were taken to see what went so terribly wrong. The crew then jettisoned the Lunar Module that had saved their lives, leaving it to burn up in the Earth's atmosphere.

On the afternoon of April 17, Apollo 13's Command Module made a nerve-wracking but successful reentry into Earth's atmosphere, allowing Lovell to consider the mission a "successful failure." Gene Kranz, the Lead Flight Controller at Mission Control, considered Apollo 13's safe return to be "NASA's finest hour," and everyone at NASA breathed a heavy sigh of relief when Apollo 13's crew made it back safely, but NASA began officially investigating what went wrong the day after splashdown, and for eight months, there were no Apollo missions, a lull about twice as long as the intervals between the previous missions.

Ultimately, Apollo 13's close call did not deter NASA from continuing manned missions to the Moon. On January 31, 1971, Apollo 14 lifted off with the exact same mission Apollo 13 had. Apollo 13 likely would have faded into relative obscurity had it successfully completed its mission, because that has largely been Apollo 14's fate. Apollo 14 successfully analyzed the Fra Mauro highlands and crater by spending over 30 hours on the Moon's surface before returning without incident, but the harrowing mission that came before it has since been the subject of a critically acclaimed movie and remains well-known over 45 years later.

The Apollo Program: The History and Legacy of America's Most Famous Space Missions analyzes the Apollo program and the events that led to the famous Moon missions. Along with pictures of important people, places, and events, you will learn about Apollo like never before.

Chapter 1: A Great New American Enterprise

"Now it is time to take longer strides - time for a great new American enterprise - time for this nation to take a clearly leading role in space achievement, which in many ways may hold the key to our future on Earth." – President Kennedy, 1961

A picture of Kennedy's address to Congress in 1961

The Apollo missions would require cutting edge rockets to launch state of the art modular spacecrafts to the Moon, while ensuring a successful reentry of the spacecraft back into Earth's atmosphere. When Kennedy outlined the vision in 1961, NASA did not yet possess the scientific or technological know-how for the spacecraft's return, and the spacecraft and rockets themselves did not exist yet.

At the beginning of the Apollo program, NASA wasn't even sure what the design would be for the spacecraft that would go to the Moon and back. At first blush, NASA's engineers assumed it would be easiest to directly launch a spacecraft to the Moon and equip it with boosters to launch it back to Earth. This approach, referred to as "direct ascent," seemed feasible to NASA because the Moon had no atmosphere, making ascent from the Moon relatively easy.

Still, a minority of NASA employees advocated other designs. One design, known as "Earth Orbit Rendezvous," would have attempted to assemble several pieces together into a spacecraft while in orbit. The "Earth Orbit Rendezvous" was used to assemble the International Space Station, but it was beyond the capabilities of NASA in the 1960s.

Meanwhile, another minority advocated what came to be known as the "Lunar Orbit Rendezvous" mission. Lunar Orbit Rendezvous required having a rocket launch a spacecraft consisting of three major components: a service module, command module and lunar module. The three modules would remain attached until the spacecraft began orbiting the Moon, at which point the lunar module detached and landed on the surface while the Command/service module orbited the Moon. The advocates for this type of mission argued that it would actually be the best option because it would require landing the least mass on the Moon. By the end of 1962, NASA was convinced that a Lunar Orbit Rendezvous mission was the best option.

Once NASA settled on using Lunar Orbit Rendezvous for the Apollo missions, they still had to design and construct the modular spacecraft and rockets. Right away, NASA faced a major logistical challenge: any lunar landing mission would require multiple crewmembers, but NASA had never developed a spacecraft that held more than one crewmember. To accomplish this, NASA designed a Command/service module. The service module would hold essentials like oxygen, water, and power, while the three astronauts would be in the command module during liftoff, orbit and reentry. The ultra-light lunar module, which was designed to descend and ascend to and from the Moon, could hold two astronauts. On ascent from the Moon, the lunar module would re-dock with the still orbiting Command/service module.

Designing the spacecraft wasn't even the hardest part. NASA also had to develop rockets capable of first launching the modular spacecraft into Earth's orbit, and then launching it toward the Moon. The Soviets struggled throughout the 1960s to design rockets up to the task, but NASA got it right with the Saturn V rocket, which to this day remains the most powerful launching rocket NASA ever used.

The companies that built each of the launch technologies epitomized the grand vision of a federal government and American public committed to funding gargantuan budgets that would send men on their way to the Moon. Each piece of hardware that would be used for a Moon mission, from the spacecraft, to the rockets, to the assembly buildings, transports, and operations headquarters, all developed into mammoth constructions. The crawler at the Saturn V rocket's base, "a great red-white-and-black skyscraper coming to life and advancing," transported the rocket to the launch pad, but essentially it was a launch pad that moved: Craig Nelson explained in *Rocket Men*:

> "As built by (Ohio's) Marion Power Shovel Company, the crawler took shape with eight tracks, each even by forty-one feet, with cleats like a Sherman tank, except that each cleat weighed a ton. Mounter over these eight tracks was the platform, bigger than a baseball diamond, on which the Apollo-Saturn V and it mobile launcher would ride VAB [Vehicle Assembly Building] to pad one mile per hour. The package weighed nine thousand tons, two-thirds cargo, one-third crawler."[1]

---

[1] *Rocket Men*, 3.

12,000 corporations came from the U.S., making up a total of 400,000 employees. Boeing built the Saturn V's behemoth bottom stage in New Orleans and barged the rocket across the Gulf of Mexico and across the canals of Florida. North American Rockwell in Seal Beach, California built Stage 2, which traveled through the Panama Canal. Stage 3 was built by Douglas in Sacramento, California, and was transported on Aero Supplies' specially modified Boeing Stratocruiser -- the "Super Guppy" -- to Kennedy Space Center. This same plane would carry the Command and Service Modules from North American's Downey, California plant, while the Lunar Module traveled by train from Grumman's factory in Bethpage, New York.[2]

The operation to build a Saturn rocket and put a spacecraft atop it involved the individual check of every part, and the manual for these checks surpassed 30,000 pages. Every machine was "tortured" in tests to produce 99.9% reliability. If the tests worked for every dial, switch, pump, light, fan, valve, and motor, Cape Canaveral could then return to its 1,700-page control plan. 300 pounds of monomethylhydrazine and nitrogen tetroxide were loaded into the Command and Lunar Modules, and by the time it was fully loaded for launch, the rocket and spacecraft weighed around 6.5 million pounds. Nelson notes, "6 million pounds of that weight was fuel and propellant: liquid oxygen (LOX) and kerosene for stage one; LOX and liquid hydrogen (LH2) for stage 2; and the hypergolics [self-igniting] for the tiny modules that in its final days would be the missions only spaceships."[3]

Despite the fact America's history of rockets, such as the Redstone and Titan, included notorious explosions on the launch pad, not a single Saturn ever blew up. That's made all the more remarkable by the size, volume, and danger involved. As Kennedy rocket scientist Bob Jone explained, "You remained on the pad while the LOX prechilled, with xenon lights, and the wind blowing, and as those pipes chill, they scream...This thing is groaning and moaning and the hydraulic pumps are coming on...We would watch that thing ignite a beautiful, absolute, thunderous roar, zillions of horsepower, and you visualize them valves workin' and them turbo pumps goin' ch-ch-ch-ch-ch-ch. The thing if smokin' and ventin' and shakin' and screamin'!"[4]

Apollo would carry men to the Moon partly because of the success of the Saturn. The rocket design signaled the intersection of a great many ideas about the future of American spaceflight and what kind of agency NASA would be. The short answer is civilian. Gemini used a military rocket, the Titan IIA, a heavy booster. The U.S. Air Force also had their hands all over the rocket, using it to launch spy satellites, and the military branch also planned to use Gemini, or Code Blue, as the missions would have been called. Military astronauts would have flown Geminis (I, II, and "Big Gemini") and docked them with Air Force spy space stations, demonstrating just how much the Cold War mentality already infected much of the U.S. space program. While there was the "Space Race," there was also the Rocket and Missile Race, and

[2] *Rocket Men*, 4.
[3] *Rocket Men*, 6-7.
[4] *Rocket Men*, 6.

that larger competition between nations, which also involved a great deal of the same technology, signaled to some the growing danger of the militarization of outer space.[5]

There was not only a competition between nations, but one between American rocket and missile scientists as well. The debate about what to do with space, either to extend the arms race into Earth orbit or let the scientists have their way, preoccupied the decision-making of President Eisenhower. On the eve of leaving the office of the presidency, he was faced with a decision to cancel the Mercury Program and not initiate a replacement. Advisors warned him of the "scientists," saying if he allowed men like Wernher Von Braun to control the space program, scientists would want to explore the solar system.

The Saturn V rocket ahead of the launch of Apollo 10

The Saturn V rockets were truly gargantuan, standing nearly 350 feet tall and holding thousands of tons of fuel. These rockets could carry a payload weighing over 250,000 pounds into orbit, giving it the ability to launch the Apollo spacecraft into orbit in about 12 minutes at

[5] *Rocket Men*, 90.

nearly 18,000 miles per hour. But that was just the beginning of the Saturn V's duties. Once in orbit, the Saturn V still had to accelerate the spacecraft to nearly 25,000 miles per hour to allow the spacecraft to escape the Earth's orbit and head for the Moon.

Designing rocket engines that powerful was hard enough, but NASA had to design the Saturn V to accomplish its duties in multiple stages, because an Apollo spacecraft typically had to spend a few hours in orbit around the Earth before heading for the Moon. Thus, the Saturn V's first two stages would accelerate the spacecraft to about 15,000 miles per hour, while the third and final stage would enter the spacecraft into Earth's orbit at about 18,000 miles per hour. But this third and final stage also had to be capable of essentially restarting and reaccelerating to propel the spacecraft out of Earth's orbit and to the Moon at about 25,000 miles per hour.

The first challenge was to get the Apollo spacecraft into orbit, which required escaping Earth's atmosphere at about 18,000 miles per hour. From the launch pad, the first stage of the Saturn V rocket would accelerate the spacecraft to over 6,000 miles per hour in two and a half minutes before detaching and falling away. The second stage accelerated the spacecraft to about 15,000 miles per hour after six more minutes before falling away.

The Saturn V's third stage was the most crucial. First, it accelerated the spacecraft to 18,000 to enter it into orbit before shutting down. The spacecraft then orbited around the Earth to wait for the Moon's orbit to properly line up for the three day voyage to the Moon's orbit. The Apollo spacecrafts usually had to orbit around Earth at least once before it was time to head to the Moon. At the speed the spacecraft was going, it would only take a few hours to orbit the entire planet.

Next, the Saturn V's third stage had to reactivate itself for the "Trans Lunar Injection," accelerating the spacecraft to about 25,000 miles per hour to reach the escape velocity necessary to escape Earth's orbit. At this time, the lunar module attached to the command/service module, and once the spacecraft reached escape velocity, the Saturn V's third stage fell away on a different trajectory.

Once the spacecraft escaped Earth's orbit, it would take three days of cruising and a short engine burst known as the "Lunar Orbit Insertion" procedure to properly position the spacecraft to be captured by the Moon's orbit. NASA had mapped the Moon during previous missions, in order to help choose the landing sites for the Apollo lunar modules. When the Moon captured the spacecraft, the spacecraft would complete several orbits around the Moon to properly line up the lunar module for descent.

To descend thousands of feet down to the Moon's surface, the lunar module had both an engine and thrusters that would allow it to maintain speed, control and direction. The lunar module would descend in a pirouette to help it descend straight. As Apollo 11's lunar module inadvertently proved, any incorrect timing or ill timed thrust would land a module several miles away from its intended destination, which could be the difference between a smooth landing or landing among boulders and craters. For most of the descent, the lunar module was automated, but the final stage of the descent required manual controls. When the descent stage was finished, it would fall away from the module, like the Saturn V rocket stages.

The Apollo astronauts usually spent between 20-36 hours on the Moon's surface, collecting several pounds of rocks and samples, and in later missions using rovers to travel around. When it was time to leave the Moon's surface, the lunar module would ascend back to re-dock with the command/service module. Since the Moon has no atmosphere, it was relatively easy for the lunar modules to ascend without needing powerful rockets like the Saturn V. The lunar module had an ascent stage with fuel propulsion engines to propel it back up to the command/service module. Once the lunar module rejoined the orbiter, the ascent stage was jettisoned, often landing back on the Moon.

The Moon's orbit is only a fraction of Earth's, so once the modules linked back up, the Command/service module was equipped with engines to propel it back toward Earth. The bigger concern for the return was that the modules had to reenter Earth's orbit at the proper angle to allow the planet to recapture it. Reentry into Earth's atmosphere subjects spacecrafts to temperatures of about 3,000 degrees Fahrenheit, so the module had an elaborate heat shield consisting of a mixture of dozens of panels, insulation and aluminum. A failure in any part of the heat shield system would be fatal.

Finally, it was time for the splashdown. The module had several "drogue parachutes," used for decelerating fast moving objects, which were used at about 25,000 feet. Those parachutes slowed the module down to about 125 miles per hour. Another set of parachutes would then slow the module down to about 20 miles per hour before it hit the water.

Once the module splashed down, divers would deploy rafts to pick up the astronauts and anchor the module while a helicopter hovered overhead to collect everyone and everything. After being picked up, the returning astronauts would be quarantined for a period of time to study the effects the mission had on their bodies.

A picture of the Apollo 1 crew practicing the splashdown and exiting the module

Most people can name Apollo 11 as the first mission to land men on the Moon, and a critically acclaimed film about Apollo 13's harrowing mission was released in 1995. As a result, the rest of the Apollo missions have been greatly overshadowed, including Apollo 8, despite the fact Apollo 8 accomplished several firsts and ultimately made Apollo 11 possible. However, none of those missions would've taken place the way they did without the bitter lessons learned by Apollo 1.

Cape Canaveral Air Force Station Launch Complex 34, site of the Apollo 1 disaster

Chapter 2: Simulated Launch

Picture of the arrival of the Apollo 1 command module

"On the morning of January 27, 1967, a test of SIC 012 commenced. The purpose of the test was to verify systems operation in a simulated launch and to exercise countdown procedures in preparation for actual launch. The test was identified as a Space Vehicle Plugs Out Integrated Test OCP FO-K-0021-1 in which the spacecraft would be electrically disconnected from the Ground Support Equipment (GSE) by removing the umbilical connectors normally disconnected at the time of launch." – Passage from the *Report of the Apollo 204 Review Board*

In a nation that was becoming increasingly bogged down in Vietnam and where Civil Rights marchers and leaders were regularly targeted for violence, the space program had become for many a shining beacon, giving hope to a nation in desperate need of something to believe in. Just a few days before the Apollo 1 disaster, a *United Press International* article had announced, "Apollo 1 astronauts Virgil (Gus) Grissom, Edward White and Roger Chaffee are set to ride a powerful Saturn rocket into orbit Feb. 21 to inaugurate the manned portion of the Apollo men-to-the-moon program. The launch date, made official Monday by the U.S. Space Agency, misses by one day the fifth anniversary of America's first orbital venture—the 5 1-2 hour flight of John Glenn in the 'Friendship 7' Mercury capsule."

White, Grissom, and Chafee posing with a model of the Command/service module

A picture of the Apollo 1 crew and the backup crew: David R. Scott, James A. McDivitt, and Russell L. Schweickart

   Known officially as AS-204, the Apollo 1 spacecraft was designed to be the first manned Command/service Module to orbit the earth for any length of time, perhaps as much as two weeks, and the confidence that both NASA and the American people had in the program could be seen in the *Command Service Module System Handbook*, published less than two weeks before the incident. According to that publication, the module had "been prepared by the Flight Control Division, Manned Spacecraft Center, Houston, Texas, with technical support by North American Aviation" and contained the following stern warning: "Information contained within this section represents the Command Service Module Systems for the AS-501 Mission as of January 16, 1967. Information as shown reflects spacecraft systems with major emphasis on material for use by Flight Controllers in real time; however, caution should be exercised in using these systems drawings for any purpose other than flight control." Ironically, although it was more than 300 pages long, it contained no information on emergency exit systems for the module.

The three men who were part of the launch rehearsal that day knew full well the potential danger of the mission and even mockingly prayed to a model of their command/service module in one parody of their official mission portrait. The commander of the mission was Virgil Grissom, known to his friends and the American public as Gus, and when asked about the danger of space travel a month before the disaster, he replied, "You sort of have to put that out of your mind. There's always a possibility that you can have a catastrophic failure, of course; this can happen on any flight; it can happen on the last one as well as the first one. So, you just plan as best you can to take care of all these eventualities, and you get a well-trained crew and you go fly." After his death, one Associated Press article observed, "For Air Force Lt. Col. Virgil I. Grissom, the first Apollo mission would have been his third trip into space, a distinction no man today can claim. … Some called Gus Grissom a hard-luck astronaut. As one of the famed original seven Mercury spacemen, he became the second American to fly in space. Taking a 15-minute sub-orbital flight July 21, 1961 he had to swim for his life when his tiny spaceship, Liberty Bell 7, blew its hatch and sank. On March 23, 1965, he and Navy Cmdr. John W. Young had the honor of launching the United States into its highly successful Gemini program with a three-orbit flight in Gemini 3. Grissom, 40, was a short man with a deep, business-like voice who wore his hair in a crewcut. Born in Mitchell, Ind., he once said he decided as a sixth grader there, watching airplanes overhead, that the flying business was for him. The Air Force turned him down because he was too young, only 17, when he first tried to enlist as a fighter pilot in World War II. He got on duty a year later, but as a typist. He married his high school sweetheart, Betty Moore, during his first leave. After the war he worked as a fry cook in a hamburger shop, while his wife worked as a telephone operator, and graduated from Purdue University. During the Korean War he finally won his wings, going on to fly 100 missions and win the Distinguished Flying Cross. He became an astronaut in 1959."

With Grissom on that fateful morning were Edward White and Roger Chaffee. Of White, the same reporter wrote, "The son of an Air Force General, White, 36, was born in San Antonio, Tex., but lived there only a short time. As a 'military brat' he was at a loss to call any place his home town. He was graduated from West Point and later earned a master's degree in aeronautical engineering from the University of Michigan. Still later he attended test pilot school at Edwards Air Force Base, Calif. A deeply religious man, White, a Methodist, attended church regularly. He kept his six-foot frame in top physical condition. In fact, he ranked No. 1 in physical aptitude in his class of 1952 at West Point, and set a 440-yard hurdle record. He married the former Patricia E. Finegan of Washington D.C., and they had a son and a daughter."

According to the article, Chaffee was born to be a pilot and "inherited his love for the air. His father, Donald Chaffee of Grand Rapids, Mich., is a former barnstormer who flew at county fairs in an open cockpit airplane. The astronaut was slight, dark-haired man who at 31 already had begun to gray. Coworkers praised him as a smart engineer. … Chaffee held a bachelor's degree in aeronautical engineering from Purdue and chose a Navy career through the ROTC program. He met his wife, Martha Horn of Oklahoma City, Okla., while at Purdue. Chaffee became an astronaut with the third group named in 1963 after a tour of duty at the Jacksonville, Fla., Naval Air Station. Part of his duty there was taking pictures of Mercury Spaceships as they soared aloft from Cape Kennedy, Fla."

A picture of the men pretending to pray to the module

The nation had much to look forward to with this latest venture, as Apollo 1 would carry a television camera, designed to send video back to NASA and to let the astronauts broadcast portions of their flight to audiences on earth. This was a vital part of NASA's public relations campaign to keep their very expensive budget intact. As the Vietnam War continued to heat up and the War on Poverty became a popular cause, some in the country were beginning to question why the government was spending so much money to send a few men into space.

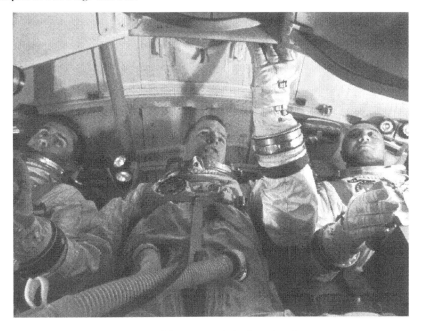

A picture of the crew training in a simulator

A picture of the crew entering the module in a previous test in 1966

"The Plugs-Out Test was initiated on January 27, 1967 at 12:55 GMT (7:55 a.m. EST) when power was applied to the spacecraft for this test. After completion of initial verification tests of system operation the flight crew entered the Command Module. ... The Command Pilot noted an odor in the Spacecraft Environmental Control System suit oxygen loop and the count was held at 18:20 GMT while a sample of the oxygen in this system was taken. This odor has been determined from subsequent analysis not to be related to the fire. ... Communication difficulties were encountered and the count was held at approximately 22:40 GMT to troubleshoot the problem. ... From 22:45 GMT until about 22:53 GMT the flight crew interchanged equipment related to the communications systems in an effort to isolate the communications system problem. ... During the troubleshooting period problems developed in the ability of various ground stations to communicate with one another and with the crew. None of the communications problems appear to have had a direct bearing on the fire." – Passage from the *Report of the Apollo 204 Review Board*

Entering 1967, the Apollo project was going well. In fact, during the previous month, NASA had decided to cancel one of its major test flights, ruling that such an expensive trip was not needed. Instead, the three man crew could focus on preparing for their February 21 launch.

On the fateful morning of January 27, they were performing the Plugs Out Integrated Test. According to the report of the Apollo 204 Review Board, "The purpose of the Space Vehicle Plugs-Out Integrated Test, Operational Checkout Procedures (OCP) FO-K-0021-1, Spacecraft 012 is to demonstrate all space vehicle systems and operational procedures in as near a flight configuration as is practical and to verify their capability in a simulated launch. System verification is performed, an abbreviated final countdown conducted and a flight simulation made. All communication and instrumentation systems are activated and proper measurements are monitored at appropriate ground stations. At the start of the simulated flight, umbilicals are disconnected and the spacecraft is on simulated fuel-cell power. Specific objectives of this test for Spacecraft 012 as stated in the Final Procedure Document were:

a) To verify overall spacecraft/launch vehicle compatibility and demonstrate proper function of spacecraft systems with all umbilicals and Ground Support Equipment disconnected.

b) To verify no electrical interference at the time of umbilical disconnect.

c) To verify astronaut emergency egress procedures (unaided egress) at the conclusion of the test."

At first, everything seemed to be functioning normally. The test began at 7:55 a.m., but when the astronauts entered the module and took their seats around 1:00 p.m., Grissom complained about smelling a strange odor that he described as a "sour smell" coming from his oxygen supply. This resulted in the simulated countdown being stopped at 1:20, but after checking it out, the men in charge determined that it was nothing to be concerned about and authorized the tests to continue. The countdown started again around 2:45 in the afternoon. When the countdown resumed, support crew stepped forward to secure the three hatches which would ultimately trap the crew in the sudden inferno.

Lewis Curatolo, from North American Aviation, helped the astronauts into their seats that fateful day and later reported, "At approximately 1300 I notified the Test Conductor and Test Project Engineer that we were ready to perform Crew ingress. The Suit Technician and the Spacecraft Technician performed the pre-ingress layout of the cockpit and couches. This procedure consists of laying out the pilots seat and shoulder harnesses, and routing of the 02 umbilical hoses. … After completion of the Crew ingress we proceeded with Hatch closeout, and Cabin purge, as directed by the Environmental Control System engineer and Test Project Engineer. … At this time we were directed to proceed with outer hatch and Boost Protective Cover closeout. We installed the outer crew hatch and started with the Boost Protective Cover installation but experienced some difficulty in getting the Boost Protective Cover to lock in, so I notified the Test Project Engineer and asked for an Interim Discrepancy Report. The Boost Protective Cover was left unlatched and we were instructed by the Test Supervisor and Test Conductor to clear the White Room. I followed the Test Conductor's instructions and at this point (1730) the 2nd shift Pad Leader (Don Babbitt) relieved me."

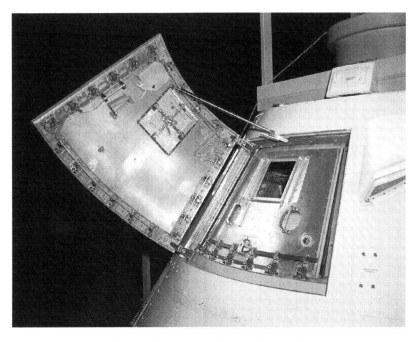

A picture of the hatch design used on Apollo 1

As if there hadn't been enough omens, the countdown had to be stopped again at 5:40 due to communication problems. The crew was wired with a live microphone that they needed to be able to turn off from time to time, but the microphone could not be turned off. While this problem was being dealt with, other activities related to the countdown continued, and at 6:20 p.m., with all other countdown functions completed, NASA decided to hold the launch clock at T-10 until the problem with the microphone could be fixed.

As much as investigators looked back again and again at the crew's final moments, no one could ever determine what exactly went wrong. The Review Board later noted, "From the start of the T-10 minute hold at 23:20 GMT until about 23:30 GMT there are no events that appear to be related to the fire. The major activity during this period was routine troubleshooting of the communications problem. The records show that except for the communications problem, all systems were operating normally during this period. There were no voice transmissions from the spacecraft from 23:30:14 GMT until the transmission reporting the fire which began at 23:31:04.7 GMT (6:31:04.7 p.m. EST)."

As far as what was going on inside the module or in the heads of those who were unwittingly facing imminent death, there is no evidence to indicate that they had any concerns. NASA took the health of its astronauts seriously and wired them with numerous sensors designed to immediately detect any sort of physical problem that might compromise the mission. Not only did these monitors constantly transmit data back to Mission Control, they also left behind records that showed how the men were doing. According to those who examined these records, "During the period beginning about 30 seconds before the report there are indications of crew movement. … There is, however, no evidence as to what this crew movement was or that it was related to the fire. The biomedical data indicate that just prior to the fire report the Senior Pilot was performing essentially no activity (or was in the baseline 'rest' condition) until about 23:30:21 GMT [6:30:21 locally] when a slight increase in pulse and respiratory rate was noted. At 23:30:30 GMT the electrocardiogram indicates some muscular activity for several seconds. Similar indications are noted at 23:30:39 GMT. The data show increased activity but are not indicative of an alarm type of response. By 23:30:45 GMT, all of the biomedical parameters had reverted to the baseline 'rest' level."

Another sensor that registered movement was the gas chromatograph cable, which would have run to the gas chromatograph had it been installed in the command module. According to the report, "When the gas chromatograph is not connected, the cable acts as an antenna. Thus, changes in the electromagnetic field within the spacecraft are sensed when the cable is approached closely, touched or moved or voltage fluctuations occur in other equipment. Variations found in the signal level from the gas chromatograph cable at earlier times in the test have been correlated with either crew movement or voltage transients when equipment was turned off or on at these earlier times. The variation at 23:30:50 GMT, may have resulted because it was touched or approached by the crew since there does not appear to be any voltage transient condition at this time which could have given the observed signal."

In essence, investigators could find nothing in the data to indicate at that point in time that the astronauts of Apollo 1 had only seconds to live.

Chapter 4: A Flash Fire

"Gus Grissom, Edward White and Roger Chaffee were killed tonight in a flash fire during tests of the Apollo Saturn 204 vehicle at Cape Kennedy AFB. The fire occurred while the astronauts were in the space craft during the countdown of simulated flight test. The accident occurred at 6:31 EST at T-10 minutes prior to the planned simulated liftoff. The spacecraft was located 218 feet above the launch pad and was mated to the uprated Saturn 1B launch vehicle. Hatches on the spacecraft were closed. Emergency crews were hampered by dense smoke removing the hatches. An unknown number of launch crew workers were treated to smoke inhalation at the Cape Kennedy dispensary. The crew had entered the spacecraft at 3 p.m. Minor difficulties had been encountered during the count with the environmental control and communications systems. All data has been impounded pending an investigation." - Official statement from NASA following the accident

Perhaps the only positive thing that can be said about the tragedy was that when the end came, it likely happened very quickly. At 6:30:54.8 local time, the machines monitoring the module noted "a significant voltage transient" in the AC Bus 2 voltage, and 10 seconds later, the men indicated there was a problem. 30 seconds after that, they were likely dead, or at least unconscious.

The tape recordings made from the astronaut's microphones show that they likely suffered for only a few seconds, though how long that time period seemed to be to them is beyond human imagination. According to an analysis made of the tapes:

"The total time duration of these two transmissions was brief, lasting 17.1 seconds; the first lasted 5.3 seconds and the second lasted 5.0 seconds, with a 6.8 second period of no transmission between… Except for a portion of the first transmission, which is quite clear, the remainder of the first and second transmission is not clear and it is impossible to define exactly what was said by the crew. … [The first] transmission began at 23:31:04.7 GMT [6:31:04.7 local time] with an exclamatory remark. … Most listeners believe this initial remark was one of the following: 'Hey ' 'Fire ' 'Break ' Most listeners believe…that this transmission was made by the Command Pilot. This remark is followed by a short period of noise (bumping sounds, etc.). … The second portion of this first transmission begins at 23:31:06.2 GMT with an unclear word. Most listeners believe the first to be one of the following: 'I 've' 'We've' The remainder of this transmission is quite clear and is: '...Got a fire in the cockpit', followed by a clipped word sounding like 'VHEH', which ended at 23:31:10 GMT. Many listeners believed this transmission to have been made by the Pilot. … The entire second transmission is somewhat garbled [and] is subject to wide variation of…The following is a list of some of the interpretations that have been made:

(1). 'Fighting a bad fire - Let's get out ..... Open 'er up.'

(2). 'We've got a bad fire - Let's get out ..... We're burning up. ' 'I'm reporting a bad fire .... I'm getting out..Oh, AAH.' (Scream)"

A. R. Caswell, who was at one of the television monitors, later testified, "At approximately 18:30 Eastern Standard Time my attention was directed to the monitor by OTV technician Gary Propst, his remarks was that there is a fire in the capsule. … Upon directing my attention to the remark by technician Propst, I observed on the white room camera, a flickering of flame inside of the capsule on the left side of the port hole. This flame flickered for some time I would estimate 15 - 20 seconds and then it spread across almost the full face of the port in the hatch cover. … Reverting my glance back again to the camera covering the hatch porthole I would estimate that some 30 to 40 seconds elapsed before the flames reached a very high proportion, in which there was nothing visible but a white searing type of flame inside the cockpit. The period specified from 15 to, or rather to, 30 to 40 seconds was subsequent to my initial time that I observed the fire in the hatch. The fire, the flames that I saw were definitely inside the capsule, there was no fire around the hatch at this particular point in time."

The men had trained for such an emergency and seem to have sprung into action to try to survive. The protocol called for White, occupying the center seat, to unlatch the inner hatch, and video recorded by the television camera gave the impression that he at least tried to do this. Caswell testified, that "when we first noticed the flames at the cockpit it appeared on the left side facing the hatch cover. And it was during this initial period that we detected what we feel was motion by some movement of the helmet of the center crew member. And then seconds perhaps 10 to 15 seconds the flames had spread across the face. …I did notice what appeared to be motion of the center crew man upon the initial outbreak of fire as my observation was directed to it. And then it appeared within perhaps 20 seconds, the flames had obscured a good view or any type of view of the crew member because they were spread across the face of the porthole. As time progressed, perhaps to 45 seconds to a minute, the intensity of the flames greatly increased to where they appeared to be white hot. This is confined to inside the spacecraft."

One thing that has troubled investigators for years is the testimony of Propst, who also watched on his video monitor as events unfolded but gave a very different time line. According to Propst, "At about 1830 one of the Astronauts said, 'Fire in the cockpit', this was followed by a scream and then silence. … Immediately I looked over to our camera 24 which is located inside the White Room. …as soon as my eyes caught sight of the camera 24 monitor I noticed a bright glow inside the spacecraft, however, I saw no flames. Just a split second later I saw flames go past the porthole. The flames were not in the order of an explosion but were, in fact, that of something just burning. The fire increased steadily during the next two to two and one half minutes. … The first thing I saw was what appeared to be the center Astronaut's arms reaching above his head toward the hatch. There followed a great deal of motion as his arms seemed to fumble with something and then quickly reach back for it. From time to time the top of his helmet could be seen. About 15 seconds after the cry of fire, I saw more arms in front of the porthole seemingly coming from the left. Looking further back into the spacecraft, I could see the legs of the center Astronaut moving about. The movement inside the spacecraft lasted about 2 minutes before the flames began to block the view. At first the flames were behind the Astronaut's arms toward the center of the spacecraft and then spread forward to the area of the hatch."

As they watched the scene unfold, Propst and his co-workers speculated about exactly what they were seeing, trying as people so often do during a disaster to wrap their minds around an incredible and unbelievable situation. He continued, "During the entire time that I watched the Astronauts' moving, their spacesuits were silver in color with no signs of being burned or charred. I think it noteworthy that no one entered the White Room until it had become smoke-filled some minutes later. Had anyone entered and gone near the spacecraft they would have been visible on the TV camera. ... I know that my times are very near accurate because I remember saying to others that had gathered in the area of the monitor: 'Blow the hatch, why don't they blow the hatch?' One person that was near said that the spacesuits would protect them from the heat until they could get out. A short conversation then took place concerning how long and how much the suits could protect them from the fire. Also comment was made on why no one had entered the White Room as yet. During the time of this conversation the White Room was still clear and the Astronaut's motion still visible."

Chapter 5: The Hatch Fell

"Gleaves who had at various times been forced to the swing arm by the smoke, returned, saw that the hatch was part way down and gave it a kick. As a result of the kick, the hatch fell even further into the Command Module. Gleaves had secured a flashlight from his tool box during one of his entries into the white room and peered into the dark smoke and soot-covered interior of the Command Module. He could see nothing except the faint glow of the floodlights mounted near the couches. The lights were within inches of his position, but they appeared to be small candles very far away. W. M. Medcalf entered the 'white room' and began his attempt to remove the inner hatch completely from the Command Module. Members of the regular fire department began arriving at Level A-8. The pad egress team, which had been standing by at the fire station, also responded to the call, but in much slower M113 Armored Personnel Carriers. The team was scheduled to participate in the egress exercise, scheduled at the end of the plugs out test." – Passage from the *Report of the Apollo 204 Review Board*

Since White likely passed out before he could open the hatch, it was left to those on the outside to try to conduct a rescue, but they were plagued with problems that prevented them from offering any timely help. When investigators asked how much time actually passed before the astronauts were reached, Donald Babbitt of North American Aviation testified to the Review Board, "The time period in here I can only estimate as 5 to 15 seconds. I heard on the head set…Mr. Chaffee say, 'There is a fire in here,' (or words to this effect). I ordered the mechanical lead man, Mr. Gleaves, to 'Get them out of there' (meaning remove the hatches and get the crew out of the Command Module)."

However, less than 20 seconds after the fire in the module broke out, the flame breached its exterior and began to spread. At this point, Babbitt realized that his own life was in danger because if the fire spread out of control, it might reach the rocket fuel and cause a detonation that would've leveled the entire launch pad. He recalled, "I started to turn toward the Communications Box (on my left), when out of the corner of my eye, I saw flame come out from under the boost near the steam duct. I almost completed my turn when I was hit by a concussion or sheet of flame (I don't remember hearing an explosion) and was pushed toward the communication boxes. My next thoughts were to get out of there. (I never had time to notify the blockhouse). I went to the umbilical (White Room) arm, [into which the hatch should open] and went across it to the umbilical tower where I encountered three of the spacecraft mechanics and an elevator talker who had a head set. I told the talker to inform the test supervisor that we were on fire and that I need firemen, ambulances, and equipment. With the three mechanics (Messrs. Gleaves, Hawkins, and Clemmons) we grabbed the only CO_2 bottle available and went back to the White Room to try to remove the hatches. The smoke and heat was so intense that we could only spend a short time in the White Room (possibly 1-2 minutes). After several trips back and forth Mr. Gleaves almost passed out due to smoke inhalation so I ordered him to stay out, which he did but for only a short time."

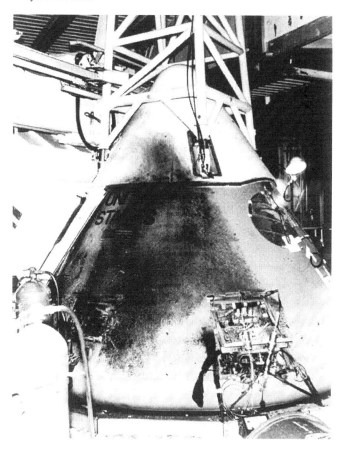

Pictures of the charred module

Crises, especially when being handled by highly trained personnel, typically begin as a highly structured and detail-oriented exercise but often progress to more and more desperate measures, as the best trained among the respondents exchange procedures for experience and initiative. So it was in the minutes that followed the Apollo 1 fire. James Gleaves, one of the first men to approach the module, later reported that "a gentleman named L. D. Reece found the oxygen masks and was handing out the oxygen masks. We had trouble locating the strip of tape on the bottom because they were painted the same color as the connector. And several times, one, two, three or four of us returned without masks and stayed as long as we could, then finally Babbitt and myself entered the white room after the fire had been extinguished by Jerry Hawkins and on all fours I crawled. I found the tool to remove the ablative hatch. I removed the ablative hatch and I didn't have a mask on at this time and I just couldn't take it no longer so I returned out and gave the tool to Jerry Hawkins, Steve Clements and L. D. Reece. And they removed the ablative hatch and L. D. Reece threw it out on level A8 and then these guys, also they had masks on, they removed the inner hatch and it was so hot they just let it drop down under the couch. So they come back out and I in return went in and kicked the inner hatch and it sort of fell down under the couch. I pushed but it was still hot and inside the spacecraft was black and filled full of smoke. You couldn't see anything at all. So I returned to A8 and out of the white room and got a flashlight and went back in and tried to see inside the spacecraft but the heat was too great and the smoke was too bad so we returned out on A8 and we continued to go back in. And as far as I can remember it took maybe 10 or 15 minutes for any fireman or any help to get to us up on the swing arm."

Within a few minutes, the fire nearest the module was under control, and Babbitt was placed in the unenviable position of opening the hatches. Babbitt was perhaps the first person to understand that due to a flawed design that would be discussed for decades, the men trapped inside never really had a chance of escape. Due to the increase in pressure inside the cabin during the fire, the hatches would never have been able to fully open. Babbitt recalled, "After the smoke had cleared some, I could see that the Spacecraft Technicians and Quality Control (NASA and NAA) had been able to get back into level A-8 and were fighting fires with everything available, so I got some more men and continued as best we could (because of the smoke and heat) to remove the hatches. We attempted to both remove the inner hatch or lower the hatch down inside the Command Module. We were not successful in removing the inner hatch and could only lower the hatch about 75 to 80% of the way because of obstructions. I was at that time only able, again because of the smoke which was considerable, to observe only two of the flight crew but could not recognize who it was. The inner hatch was extremely hot and we could only handle it with the handles attached to the hatch. My observation at the time of hatch removal was that the flight crew were dead and that the destruction inside the Command Module was considerable."

There was little he could now do for the men who only moments before had been his co-workers, but Babbitt carried on with his duty before finally succumbing to his own injuries. "After informing the test supervisor of what I had observed (while adhering to security guidelines wherever possible) and continued to direct the crew in putting out the fires. I asked the senior Pan American firemen to specifically check the Launch Escape Motor for hot spots and general heat. I was relieved by Mr. Curatolo, NAA 1st shift pad leader. I proceeded down the umbilical tower elevator, met the two NASA doctors and briefed them on what they would find. I then proceeded to the Pan American Dispensary, with a short stop at the NAA Shop Trailer, for treatment and checkup. I was treated for smoke inhalation, flash burns, and eye irritation, and ordered to remain overnight."

On February 8, Babbitt was called back to testify as to what he observed when he opened the hatch. He described the gruesome scene in vivid detail:

"When the inner hatch was first lowered, the only thing that I could observe was smoke inside. We could only feel the flight crew. We could not see them very well as I could tell. As the men working with me went out because they'd been in the smoke quite a while, I went back in, oh, approximately one minute or a minute and a half later; and all that I could observe was what appeared to be Mr. White laying on his back with his arms over his head, appeared to be reaching for the hatch or in something in that vicinity. I also observed what appeared to be Mr. Grissom laying with one of his arms through and appeared to be reaching in the direction of the hatch also.

I went out again for a short bit and came back in maybe thirty seconds after that. I could see a little bit more. The smoke had cleared some more. All that I could really see was, oh maybe, to the waist of Mr. White. ...I at first got the impression that they were off the seats; and then I got the impression that no they were on the seats. It appeared that their suits were shredded. I could see bare skin. ... The crew appeared to me to be in their normal, in-flight position. I could only see what appeared to be Mr. Grissom's left arm reaching through Mr. White's arm. I could not see his body that well, but it had the appearance of being in its satisfactory or its normal position. I did not observe Mr. Chaffee because I was a little bit too far to the right of the hatch and could not see him. Mr. White appeared to me to be as I say, laying in his normal boost position. I could not tell whether his head rest was up or down. In fact, I couldn't even see his features because of the, what appeared the smoke or soot blackened face plate on his helmet."

Lewis Curatolo, who had earlier helped the men into their seats and himself helped seal the hatches, recalled, "I observed that the body of the Senior Pilot was wedged between the Crew Couches and the hatch bulkhead; the Command Pilot was positioned in the center couch with his body partially hanging over the center couch. The Pilot was in a reclining position in the Pilot's Couch. I observed that the Command Pilot's leg pans were in the rest position, the Senior Pilot's leg pans were in the boost position, and the Pilot's leg pans were in the full down position."

Chapter 6: The Fire Department

"Shortly after the report of fire, a call was made to the fire department. From log records, it appears that the fire apparatus and personnel were dispatched at about 23:32 GMT. After hearing the report of the fire, the doctor monitoring the test from the blockhouse near the pad proceeded to the base of the umbilical tower. The exact time at which firemen reached Level A-8 is not known. Personnel who opened the hatches unanimously state that all hatches were open before any firemen were seen on the level or in the White Room. The first firemen who reached Level A-8 state that all hatches were open, but that the inner hatch was inside the Command Module, when they arrived. This places arrival of the firemen after 23:36 GMT. It is estimated, on the basis of tests, that seven to eight minutes were required to travel from the fire station to the launch complex and to ride the elevator from the ground to Level A-8. Thus, the estimated time of firemen arrival at level A-8 is shortly before 23:40 GMT." – Passage from the *Report of the Apollo 204 Review Board*

James Burch was one of the firemen sent over that evening, and with the fire already extinguished, their first priority was to try to rescue the astronauts. He later testified, "From the time we received the call, I would estimate that we got to the gantry in around five or six minutes. We took the slow elevator up. The fast elevator was out. It took us approximately two minutes to reach the top of the gantry. Assistant Chief, McMillan, Bob Batts the Crew Chief, Rector - Fire Fighter, Dawes the Fireman and myself reached the top. As we reached the top, I went around to the side of the capsule where the man on the headset was hollering that the men were still inside the capsule. I was not sure who was inside, and I asked him specifically who was inside the capsule. He said that the astronauts were still inside. There were about five or six technicians standing on the gangway; and as I looked into the hatch, there were two men coming out that had been working on the hatch. Me and one other fireman, I'm not sure who he was - it, I believe, was Rector, we proceeded in without a mask and tried to take the hatch cover off. It was loose but was still intact. As we picked it up and down, we couldn't move it. We jammed it back and forth quite a few times, but the smoke was thick and we did not know how to take it off."

Burch's reference itself would confuse many by giving some the impression that the hatch was still on when the firemen arrived. However, a careful reading of his remarks shows that the hatch was open and Babbitt and Cuartolo were emerging when he arrived. Thus, he was not trying to open the hatch but remove it. Many other questions would also be asked about why there were not items in place when they were needed, as well as why the "fast elevator" was not in service that day. While corrections would be made, they obviously came too late for the three men trapped inside the module.

Meanwhile, those around them could only do the best they could under the circumstances. Burch continued, "I would say we stayed in around thirty seconds before we had to leave to get a mask because the smoke was too thick. Upon going out on the gangway, one of the men out there gave me a mask - gas mask - I put it on and entered the room again with one of the technicians. We then tried again to take the hatch cover completely off. He was trying to tell me that you had to drop it down and push it in and turn it sideways to get it off. We worked quite a few minutes on trying to do that. It seemed like minutes...I'm not sure how long it was. But, anyway, we could not get it; and we were choking up considerably on the smoke and fumes that were in there. We then went back outside, got a breath of air and then returning back, we tried again to get the hatch cover off. I know I choked up two or three more times, and the man that was with me also choked up. It wasn't but just a few seconds that he choked up so bad that he turned around and left."

In spite of the physical suffering they personally experienced that day, nothing was as frustrating as the problems they had trying to gain entry into the module, and nothing as disturbing as what they found once they made it inside. Burch remembered, "Frantically, I was still working on the hatch cover. I was shaking it, turning it, doing everything in the world I could to get it off. Then, just all at once it seemed to fall back on me; and as I turned with the hatch in my hand halfway off - someone was there to grab hold of one of the handles; and we set it back away from the hatch. Then, I took a flashlight, I laid over inside the capsule trying to see the bodies or anything that I could see. The inside was burnt considerably, there were wires hanging down. I shined the light completely around inside the capsule, and I couldn't see anything except burnt wires hanging down. I then backed out, told the man on the headset, I said, 'There's no one in there.' He said, 'There has to be someone in there. They are still in there. Get them out.'"

At this defining moment, Burch faced what was likely the worst moment of his career. "I re-entered, looked around again; and I still didn't see anyone but there under me was a boot. I grabbed the boot, pulled it, it came off. There wasn't anything there except just a black mask. Then, I just grabbed an armload of I don't know what; but it seemed like it was coming loose. The first thing I knew I had a pair of legs in my hand. The hair was still intact on the legs. They were not, burnt bad. In fact, they were not burnt at all it looked to me like. I checked to see if the skin was going to slip, it wasn't so I reached my arm through both legs, under both legs, and pulled up just as hard as I could pull. The body moved probably six inches or less, but I knew I couldn't move him out. I then backed off to see just exactly what I did have. I could see that the, just the knees were sticking up on the only person that I could recognize. As far as the rest of it, it was just a black mass and I couldn't tell which way the bodies were laying or anything. I then backed out. I told the man on the headset, 'They are all dead, the fire is extinguished. The only thing we need now is to get the smoke cleared out, and then we can tell more about it.'"

In concluding his remarks, Burch offered a final observation about his experience, and how he completed his search: "As I leaned in with the light, I crawled into the hatch and went as far as my knees, I looked around with the flashlight all the way to the back of the capsule; and I could not see anyone. At the time, the knees of the top man must have been under my stomach because I drew myself back and just grabbed a hand full of which just had to be a burnt suit and came up with a pair of knees. They had to be right at the hatch. As I leaned in, I must have been lying right on top of the knees. I could not see anyone in the back, but I could see full vision all the way to the back of the capsule."

While each witness would have his own opinion about how much time had passed at this point, audio recordings would later confirm that less than 10 minutes passed between the time of the first fire report and the moment that the final hatch was opened.

Chapter 7: Resuscitation Was Impossible

"Medical opinion, based upon autopsy reports, concluded that chances of resuscitation decreased rapidly once consciousness was lost (about 15 to 30 seconds after the first suit failed) and that resuscitation was impossible by 23:36 GMT. Cerebral hypoxia, due to cardiac arrest resulting from myocardial hypoxia, caused a loss of consciousness. Factors of temperature, pressure, and environmental concentrations of carbon monoxide, carbon dioxide, oxygen, and pulmonary irritants were changing rapidly. The combined effect of these environmental factors dramatically increased the lethal effect of any factor by itself. Because it was impossible to integrate the variables with the dynamic physiological and metabolic conditions they produced, a precise time when consciousness was lost and death supervened could not be conclusively determined." – Passage from the *Report of the Apollo 204 Review Board*

The doctors arrived a few minutes later, and while everyone who had seen the bodies had to figure it was too late, there might have been some hope among the medical professionals that something could still be done before they actually arrived. However, any hope was soon gone. According to the medical panel, "The two NASA physicians and the Pan American physician then proceeded to the spacecraft. The time of arrival at the White Room on the 8th level is estimated at 6:45 pm EST (23:45 GMT). When the physicians first arrived, the hatches had been removed, the spacecraft was still smoldering, pyrotechnics had not been safetied and smoke was too thick to spend any time in the vicinity without a breathing apparatus. After a quick evaluation, it was decided that nothing could be gained by attempting immediate egress and resuscitation. By this time, some 12 to 15 minutes had elapsed since the fire began. It was evident that the crew had not survived the heat, smoke, and thermal burns. Conditions within the spacecraft (later confirmed by toxicological determinations) were such as to produce high levels of carbon monoxide (CO), carbon dioxide (C02), and other toxic gases and irritants. Also, oxygen was markedly depleted after the rupture of the spacecraft. These conditions would have necessitated institution of resuscitative measures within a very few minutes, since under optimal conditions, resuscitation commenced more than four minutes after cardiac arrest is usually unrewarding."

Knowing there was nothing they could do, the doctors joined the growing crowd of those lingering around the disaster area. "The three physicians then returned to ground level until adequate ventilation could be established. Shortly thereafter, they returned to the spacecraft with equipment for an attempted removal. After trying to remove the Senior Pilot by cutting his suit umbilicals and electrical connections, it became apparent that extensive fusion of the suits to molten nylon from the spacecraft would make removal very difficult. For this reason, it was decided to discontinue efforts at removal in the interest of accident investigation and attempt to get photographs of the spacecraft and relative positions of the crewmen before evidence was disarranged. The two NASA physicians remained in the vicinity of the spacecraft while the Pan American physician returned to ground level. NASA Security arranged for photographic coverage. After this was accomplished, one of the NA SA physicians returned to the blockhouse for approval to resume egress operations. Approval was received from Major General Samuel C. Phillips, U.S. Air Force/Apollo Program Manager, shortly after midnight, local time, and egress was begun at approximately 12:30 am EST (05:30 GMT), January 28, 1967."

As mentioned above, the doctors performing their duties knew that there would be an extensive autopsy, and that the findings had the potential to prevent a future disaster. Therefore, though exhausted with grief and effort, they made sure the astronauts' bodies made it safely into the waiting ambulances for transport to their next destination. "The Pan American Dispensary log indicates that the ambulance with the Senior Pilot arrived at the Pan American Dispensary at 1:17 am EST (06:16 GMT). The ambulance with the Command Pilot arrived at 1:35 am EST (06:35 GMT) and the ambulance with the Pilot arrived at 2:08 am EST (07:08 GMT). Therefore, removal of the crew took approximately 90 minutes and was completed about seven and a half hours after the accident. The crewmen were removed to the Bioastronautics Operational Support Unit for postmortem examinations at 4:17 am EST (09:17 GMT)."

Few forms of death strike terror in the hearts of people like that of being burned alive. In the mid-1960s, when many homes still used fire as a source of heat for at least part of the year, these types of deaths were more common and thus more feared, so when word spread that the astronauts had perished in a blazing inferno, there were both gasps of horror and questions about how much they suffered and for how long. In fact, such questions continue to this very day among those who never accepted NASA's findings.

That said, the doctors were clear when they wrote that, in all three cases, "carbon monoxide poisoning is the most significant finding." The doctors went on to say that Grissom was the most severely burned, "estimated as 60% total body surface area (36% third degree)." White suffered burns "estimated as 48% total body surface area, (40% third degree)," and Chaffee was burned on "29% total body surface area (23% third degree)." While none of the men would have died immediately from the burns, the doctors admitted they were "considered as a contributory cause of death."

Despite the horrific extent of the burns, it still seems unlikely that any of the men suffered for long. In each case, the medical panel concluded, "Loss of consciousness was due to cerebral hypoxia due to cardiac arrest, due to myocardial hypoxia. Factors of temperature, pressure and environmental concentrations of carbon monoxide, carbon dioxide, oxygen and pulmonary irritants were changing at extremely rapid rates. … The combined effect of these environmental factors dramatically increased the lethal effect of any factor by itself. It is estimated that consciousness was lost between 15 and 30 seconds after the first suit failed. Chances of re-suscitation decreased rapidly thereafter and were irrevocably lost within four minutes."

No one will ever know the sequence of events with certainty, but the medical panel did come up with something of a timeline indicating that, based on the biomedical readings, the astronauts became aware of the fire at around 6:31:04 and that at least one of the men was still conscious 42 seconds later. Beyond that, the panel also found that the "Command Pilot had moved from his normal position after the onset of fire. The suit failed prior to rupture of the pressure vessel (the time of spacecraft rupture has been estimated by Panel 5 to be 6:31:19 pm EST (23:31:19 GMT). … The Senior Pilot did not leave his position until his restraining straps were burned through. He had moved from his normal position after the onset of fire. … There is no evidence that the Pilot moved from his normal position after the start of the fire. This is consistent with the emergency egress procedure which calls for the Pilot to be the last to the leave the spacecraft."

After extensive investigation, NASA concluded, "It was most likely that the fire began in the lower forward portion of the left equipment bay, to the left of the command pilot, and considerably below the level of his couch. … The first stage, with its associated rapid temperature rise and increase in cabin pressure, terminated 15 seconds after the verbal report of fire. At this time, 23:31:19 GMT, the command module cabin ruptured. During this first stage, flames moved rapidly from the point of ignition, traveling along debris traps installed in the command module to prevent items from dropping into equipment areas during tests or flight. … The fire was not intense until about 23:31:12 GMT. … The original flames rose vertically and then spread out across the cabin ceiling. The debris traps provided not only combustible material and a path for the spread of the flames, but also firebrands of burning molten nylon. … By 23:31:12 GMT, the fire had broken from its point of origin. A wall of flames extended along the left wall of the module, preventing the command pilot, occupying the left couch, from reaching the valve that would vent the command module to the outside atmosphere."

The second and third stages were worse, but also shorter. According to NASA's findings, "Rupture of the command module marked the beginning of the brief second stage of the fire. This stage was characterized by the period of greatest conflagration due to the forced convection that resulted from the outrush of gases through the rupture in the pressure vessel. The swirling flow scattered firebrands throughout the crew compartment, spreading fire. This stage of the fire ended at approximately 23:31:25 GMT. This third stage was characterized by rapid production of high concentrations of carbon monoxide. Following the loss of pressure in the command module and with fire now throughout the crew compartment, the remaining atmosphere quickly became deficient in oxygen so that it could not support continued combustion. Unlike the earlier stages where the flame was relatively smokeless, heavy smoke now formed and large amounts of soot were deposited on most spacecraft interior surfaces as they cooled. The third stage of the fire could not have lasted more than a few seconds because of the rapid depletion of oxygen. It was estimated that the command module atmosphere was lethal by 23:31:30 GMT, five seconds after the start of the third stage."

The doctors also weighed in on why the men died so quickly, including what problems within the module itself contributed to their deaths. They maintained "that the fire originated in the cabin rather than in the suit circuit." They also agreed that the fire "was most intense on the Command Pilot's side of the spacecraft," and the suits "were not capable of providing crew protection in a fire of this intensity." Finally, they noted, "Rescue personnel were inadequately equipped for a fire-type rescue."

Chapter 8: The Personal Tragedy

A picture of the Apollo 1 medallion, one of which was carried on Apollo 9

"By authority of the Administrator, National Aeronautics and Space Administration, the Apollo 204 Review Board was established January 27, 1967. This action was initiated through oral instructions issued by the Deputy Administrator, followed by written confirmation February 3, 1967, setting forth, in detail, the broad powers and responsibilities of the Board. The Review Board convened at Kennedy Space Center (KSC), Florida, on January 28, 1967, under the Chairmanship of Dr. Floyd L. Thompson, Director of the Langley Research Center. The sessions and organized activities of the Board continued at KSC until the Board submitted its Report. During this period an intensive review was carried out in accordance with the responsibilities placed on the Board by the Administrator. A principal element of this Review was the creation of 21 Task Panels manned by experts in their respective fields. The report of these Task Panels provided the main source of information from which the Board has formulated its findings and recommendations. Periodic interim reports were provided to the Administrator. With completion of this report, the Board has been recessed subject to being reconvened at the call of the Chairman." – Passage from the *Report of the Apollo 204 Review Board*

Naturally, Americans of all stripes wanted to know what happened with Apollo 1 and why. For one thing, sabotage was considered a real possibility by many; the Space Race with the Russians was a very heated affair, so it seemed perfectly plausible that they might do something to stop American progress. There were also allegations that NASA officials were incompetent, and that someone somewhere failed to do their job properly. Finally, there was the matter of financing, as NASA was coming under increased scrutiny to actually land a man on the moon. Many understandably wondered how the space agency could get an astronaut to the Moon and back if it couldn't even protect its astronauts on the ground here.

Of course, NASA not only had the responsibility to answer the questions but plenty of motive to do so in a satisfactory manner. Within minutes of the accident being reported, NASA sent in security personnel to secure Launch Complex 34, where the fire had taken place, but once the men were determined to be dead, there was no more hurry and investigators took their time in documenting the scene and everything in it. According to NASA's final report, "Small groups of NASA and North American Aviation management, Apollo 204 Review Board members, representatives, and consultants inspected the exterior of Spacecraft 012…A detailed inspection of the spacecraft interior was then performed, followed by the preparation and approval by the Board of a command module disassembly plan." Following this plan, the entire module was packed up and shipped to a hanger at the Kennedy Space Center on February 1. Over the next several weeks, it was dismantled, piece by piece, with every item and spacecraft components being carefully photographed and studied as it was being removed. As NASA later reported, "All interfaces such as electrical connectors, tubing joints, physical mounting of components, etc. were closely inspected and photographed immediately prior to, during, and after disassembly. Each item removed from the command module was appropriately tagged, sealed in clean plastic containers, and transported under the required security to bonded storage."

By March 27, 1967, the module had been completely disassembled and thousands of its pieces had been photographed and catalogued. Throughout the process, the priority remained the same: determine what caused the fire. According to the board's Final Report, "Throughout the disassembly operation, experts meticulously studied the exposed portions of the Command Module. The relative consumption of combustibles and sooting patterns were studied for clues as to the site of the ignition source. All structural elements, covers and panels were examined for evidence of association with the ignition. Component systems and parts were studied inch by inch with magnifying glasses and frequently parts were taken into the laboratory for microscopic or metallurgical analysis. Wire bundles were given particular attention and after separation, the individual wires were examined under 7-power magnification for sites of possible arcing. All components that showed evidence of abnormal fire effects were examined internally and many were tested for functionality. Many components showed burning of internal insulation or plotting material but in all cases they were exonerated on the basis of direction of flame travel or on the basis that there could be no communication with combustibles outside the component. Particularly suspect components were disassembled for detailed examination and analysis. All of the data developed by these visual and laboratory examinations were coordinated in making the final analysis as to probable ignition sources."

Meanwhile, another team was busy analyzing the data they had collected, beginning by creating a timeline based on "significant data that were obtained just prior to the report of the fire by the astronaut crew. These time lines cover the period of one minute before the fire report until all data signals were lost. The data shown includes signals from the gas chromatograph channel, the voltage of the AC Bus 2, the C-band beacon, the VHF telemetry carrier, the flow of oxygen into the suit loop, various indicators of spacecraft motion, the biomedical data from the Senior Pilot, and audio signals (voice and noise) received on the S-band communication link. An analysis of each item and a summary of their correlation follows."

After extensive and meticulous study, the Board asserted that "30 and 45 seconds prior to the report of fire, both the Command Pilot and Senior Pilot were active. The nature and level of the activity remain unknown. Except for the transients in data measurements that occurred approximately 9 seconds prior to the report of the fire, there are no other identified relevant events that preceded the fire. It should be noted that these data transients and subsequent activity of the crew may as easily be associated with the result of the fire as with the cause. The increase in oxygen flow to the suit loop prior to and immediately following the report of the fire and its effect on the pressure distribution within the suit loop is the result of normal demand regulator response to oxygen leaking from the circuit to the cabin. This is further compounded by the response of the regulator to the rise in cabin pressure."

The report went on to draw a number of conclusions, including that the fire was most likely caused by "an electrical arc in the sector between -Y and +Z spacecraft axes. The exact location…is [likely] near the floor in the lower forward section of the left-hand equipment bay where Environmental Control System (ECS) instrumentation power wiring leads into the area between the Environmental Control Unit (ECU) and the oxygen panel. No evidence was discovered that suggested sabotage." Furthermore, the investigators described the test conditions as "extremely hazardous" and admitted that the "rapid spread of fire caused an increase in pressure and temperature which resulted in rupture of the Command Module and creation of a toxic atmosphere. Death of the crew was from asphyxia due to inhalation of toxic gases due to fire. A contributory cause of death was thermal burns…unconsciousness occurred rapidly and that death followed soon thereafter."

Perhaps the most disturbing finding was that the men likely never had a chance of survival since they were "never capable of effecting emergency egress because of the pressurization before rupture and their loss of consciousness soon after rupture." To avoid a similar occurrence, the committee recommended "the time required for egress of the crew be reduced and the operations necessary for egress be simplified."

The committee also asserted, "Adequate safety precautions were neither established nor observed for this test." They based this conclusion on the following list of problems:

- "Those organizations responsible for the planning, conduct and safety of this test failed to identify it as being hazardous. Contingency preparations to permit escape or rescue of the crew from an internal Command Module fire were not made."
- "No procedures for this type of emergency had been established either for the crew or for the spacecraft pad work team."
- "The emergency equipment located in the White Room and on the spacecraft work levels was not designed for the smoke condition resulting from a fire of this nature."
- "Emergency fire, rescue and medical teams were not in attendance."
- "Both the spacecraft work levels and the umbilical tower access arm contain features such as steps, sliding doors and sharp turns in the egress paths which hinder emergency operations."

In response, the committee made a list of recommendations:

- "Management continually monitor the safety of all test operations and assure the adequacy of emergency procedures"
- "All emergency equipment (breathing apparatus, protective clothing, deluge systems, access arm, etc.) be reviewed for adequacy"
- "Personnel training and practice for emergency procedures [should] be given on a regular basis and reviewed prior to the conduct of a hazardous operation and that service structures and umbilical towers [should] be modified to facilitate emergency operations."

The committee also found the communication system "unsatisfactory" and suggested it be improved. They further called for studies to be done to see if the atmosphere within the module could be reduced from pure oxygen to some breathable mixture that was less flammable.

In all, the Review Board found a number of what they termed "deficiencies" in the "Command Module['s] design, workmanship and quality control." These included the following:

- "Components of the Environmental Control System installed in Command Module 012 had a history of many removals and of technical difficulties including regulator failures, line failures and Environmental Control Unit failures. The design and installation features of the Environmental Control Unit make removal or repair difficult."

- "Coolant leakage at solder joints has been a chronic problem."
- "The coolant is both corrosive and combustible."
- "Deficiencies in design, manufacture, installation, rework and quality control existed in the electrical wiring."
- "No vibration test was made of a complete flight-configured spacecraft."
- "Spacecraft design and operating procedures currently require the disconnecting of electrical connections while powered."
- "No design features for fire protection were incorporated."

In response to these and other findings, the Review Board made the following suggestions:

- "An in-depth review of all elements, components and assemblies of the Environmental Control System be conducted to assure its functional and structural integrity and to minimize its contribution to fire risk."
- "Present design of soldered joints in plumbing be modified to increase integrity or the joints be replaced with a more structurally reliable configuration."
- "Deleterious effects of coolant leakage and spillage be eliminated."
- "Review of specifications be conducted, 3-dimensional jigs be used in manufacture of wire bundles and rigid inspection at all stages of wiring design, manufacture and installation be enforced."
- "Vibration tests be conducted of a flight-configured spacecraft."
- "The necessity for electrical connections or disconnections with power on within the crew compartment be eliminated."
- "Investigation be made of the most effective means of controlling and extinguishing a spacecraft fire. Auxiliary breathing oxygen and crew protection from smoke and toxic fumes be provided."

All of the analyses made clear that NASA needed to fix the command module, not only because of potential problems on the ground but also ones that might take place in space. As the report pointed out, "Once the Command Module has left the earth's environment the occupants are totally dependent upon it for their safety. It follows that protection from fire as a hazard involves much more than a quick egress. The latter has merit only during test periods on earth when the Command Module is being readied for its mission and not during the mission itself. The risk of fire must be faced; however, that risk is only one factor pertaining to the reliability of the Command Module that must receive adequate consideration. Design features and operating procedures that are intended to reduce the fire risk must not introduce other serious risks to mission success and safety."

Chapter 9: To Pursue the Exploration of Space

"The Nation's space program requires that man and machine achieve the highest capability to pursue the exploration of space. Three gallant men lost their lives in the line of duty during the development of that capability. The Apollo 204 Review Board was charged with the responsibility of reviewing the circumstances surrounding the accident, reporting its findings relating to the cause of the accident, and formulating recommendations so that inherent hazards are reduced to a minimum. Throughout its proceedings, the Board recognized the need for an impartial and totally objective review in order to arrive at its findings. The Board believes that this was accomplished. The Board is very concerned that its description of the defects in the Apollo Program that led to the condition existing at the time of the Apollo 204 accident will be interpreted as an indictment of the entire manned space flight program and a castigation of the many people associated with that program. Nothing is further from the Board's intent. The function of the Board has been to search for error in the largest and most complex research and development program ever undertaken. This report, rather than presenting a total picture of that program, is concerned with the deficiencies uncovered." – Passage from the *Report of the Apollo 204 Review Board*

Webb and other NASA officials testifying before Congress

In addition to NASA's internal investigations, the United States Senate also held hearings to determine what went wrong and what should be changed in the future. With typical political tact, the Senate committee reported, "The committee recommends that NASA continue to move the Apollo program forward to achieve its goal. ... The Apollo 204 accident, however, may well cause the date for an American landing on the moon to be accomplished early in the next decade outside the schedule set in 1961. That would be regrettable. When set in 1961, it was a goal set for achievement and it was technically feasible. While this goal had attracted a great deal of attention in terms of national prestige, as pacesetter for the program and as rallying point for the people on the program, its true significance is seldom mentioned. The target date was and still is essential to efficient management of the program. It is essential to the planning process and to maintain a vigorous and competent organization. Any program and particularly the largest and most complex research and development program ever undertaken by man—the Apollo program—must have scheduled goals. The schedule is an essential and significant management tool—without it the program would require more and more time and more and more money."

The men on the committee knew they had to walk a fine line regarding what they wrote because their findings would likely be read with more interest than those of the average Senate committee. They also had to strike a balance between respecting the lives lost and casting blame, especially on one of the nation's most popular programs. "Safety must be considered of paramount importance in the manned space flight program even at the expense of target dates. The earnest declaration that "safety is our prime consideration" must be transfused into watchfulness so that people do not again stumble into the pitfall of complacency. NASA's creation of a Flight Safety Office with broadened capabilities and better lines of communication is a step in that direction. The Congress, in the National Aeronautics and Space Administration's fiscal year 1968 authorization act, directed the Administrator to appoint an Aerospace Safety Advisory Panel to review NASA's operational plans and advise the Administrator with respect to the hazards of proposed or existing facilities, proposed operations, and on the adequacy of [proposed or existing safety standards. The committee urges NASA to continue its post-accident efforts to achieve a high degree of safety in all of its operations and we recommend that NASA utilize the above-mentioned organizations to achieve the primacy in safety desired."

Still, there was one more piece that had to be dealt with: the Senate's own right and responsibility to oversee any government institution. Therefore, the committee concluded its remarks with a fair but firm warning: "Finally, the committee urges that the National Aeronautics and Space Administration keep the appropriate congressional committees informed on significant problems arising in its programs. During the hearings it was found that late in 1965 NASA found serious problems with the contractor's management of the contracts for the Apollo command and service module spacecraft and S-II stage—the second stage of the Saturn V vehicle. Notwithstanding that in NASA's judgment the contractor later made significant progress in overcoming the problems, the committee believes it should have been informed of the situation. The committee does not object to the position of the Administrator of NASA, that all details of Government/contractor relationships should not be put in the public domain. However, that position in no way can be used as an argument for not brining this or other serious situations to the attention of the committee."

Eventually, NASA was able to use what it learned from the disaster to make effective changes to the designs of the Apollo spacecraft. As one report later admitted, "As a result of the investigation, major modifications in design, materials, and procedures were implemented. The two-piece hatch was replaced by a single quick-operating, outward opening crew hatch made of aluminum and fiberglass. The new hatch could be opened from inside in seven seconds and by a pad safety crew in 10 seconds. Ease of opening was enhanced by a gas-powered counterbalance mechanism. The second major modification was the change in the launch pad spacecraft cabin atmosphere for pre-launch testing from 100 percent oxygen to a mixture of 60 percent oxygen and 40 percent nitrogen to reduce support of any combustion. The crew suit loops still carried 100 percent oxygen. After launch, the 60/40 mix was gradually replaced with pure oxygen until cabin atmosphere reached 100 percent oxygen at 5 pounds per square inch. This 'enriched air' mix was selected after extensive flammability tests in various percentages of oxygen at varying pressures."

There were a number of other less dramatic but important changes made to the module, including "substituting stainless steel for aluminum in high-pressure oxygen tubing, armor plated water-glycol liquid line solder joints, protective covers over wiring bundles, stowage boxes built of aluminum, replacement of materials to minimize flammability, installation of fireproof storage containers for flammable materials, mechanical fasteners substituted for gripper cloth patches, flameproof coating on wire connections, replacement of plastic switches with metal ones, installation of an emergency oxygen system to isolate the crew from toxic fumes, and the inclusion of a portable fire extinguisher and fire-isolating panels in the cabin."

NASA also used what it learned from the Apollo 1 fire to make improvements to Launch Complex 34. Among those were "structural changes to the White Room for the new quick-opening spacecraft hatch, improved firefighting equipment, emergency egress routes, emergency access to the spacecraft, purging of all electrical equipment in the White Room with nitrogen, installation of a hand-held water hose and a large exhaust fan in the White Room to draw smoke and fumes out, fire-resistant paint, relocation of certain structural members to provide easier access to the spacecraft and faster egress, addition of a water spray system to cool the launch escape system (the solid propellants could be ignited by extreme heat), and the installation of additional water spray systems along the egress route from the spacecraft to ground level."

While these and other changes made the space program safer, no one would ever describe it as completely safe, any more than one might describe air travel or driving a car as completely safe. It was only possible for those in charge to minimize the risks while maximizing the rewards, and of course, the rewards were ultimately great. On July 20, 1969, two and a half years after the Apollo 1 tragedy, NASA scored its greatest success to date when Neil Armstrong and Buzz Aldrin finally planted their boots on the Moon as members of Apollo 11. One of the items Armstrong carried that day was a diamond-studded pin intended to fly with Apollo 1 and subsequently given to the agency by the three astronauts' widows.

MICHAEL J ADAMS

VIRGIL "GUS" GRISSOM
EDWARD H WHITE II
ROGER B CHAFFEE

IN MEMORY

OF

THOSE WHO MADE THE ULTIMATE SACRIFICE
SO OTHERS COULD REACH FOR THE STARS

AD ASTRA PER ASPERA
(A ROUGH ROAD LEADS TO THE STARS)

GOD SPEED TO THE CREW

OF

APOLLO 1

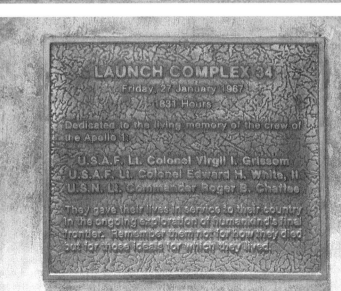

LAUNCH COMPLEX 34

Friday, 27 January 1967
1831 Hours

Dedicated to the living memory of the crew of
the Apollo 1:

U.S.A.F. Lt. Colonel Virgil I. Grissom
U.S.A.F. Lt. Colonel Edward H. White, II
U.S.N. Lt. Commander Roger B. Chaffee

They gave their lives in service to their country
in the ongoing exploration of humankind's final
frontier. Remember them not for how they died
but for those ideals for which they lived.

Pictures of memorials to the Apollo 1 crew at Cape Canaveral

A modern picture of the launch pedestal used by Apollo 1

Chapter 10: Apollo Missions Before Apollo 11

Already by late 1961, NASA had begun to mention the "Lunar Excursion Module" (LEM) as the agency's choice to land men on the Moon. Events worked quickly to decide once and for all where the LEM would rendezvous with the other spacecraft, and when NASA confirmed the ascendance of LOR, the development of the LEM commenced in full. "Considerable analytical and experimental work was underway on engineering problems associated with landing the LEM on the Moon. Landing loads and stability were studied by dropping dynamically scaled models on simulated lunar soil and by computer runs which utilized mathematical models of both the LEM and the lunar surface. At the same time an effort was underway to deduce in engineering terms the surface characteristics and soil mechanics of the lunar surface. Only the sparse photographic information from Ranger [space probe] was available to the engineers, yet later data from Surveyor and Orbiter [space probes] led to no significant change in the LEM design."[6]

Apollo proceeded on pace, and what some would call a rushed pace; to keep pace with Gemini and maintain the ambitious schedule of goals, the Command Service Module (CSM) and LEM were sped along. The program meant for its maiden flight to carry three astronauts, quite a risk

---

[6] *The Apollo Spacecraft - A Chronology*, Volume III, "Forward," Brooks, Courtney G. and Ivan D. Ertel, October 1, 1964 - January 20, 1966 (NASA SP-4009, 1973). http://www.hq.nasa.gov/office/pao/History/SP-4009/frwrd3.htm

given the new technologies under use. But as each successive stage of the Saturn rocket shot into space, each uncrewed launch of mockups and different capsule mockups only put more pressure on the deadline to launch a manned Apollo flight. The authors of *The Apollo Spacecraft* explained, "While the Mercury and Gemini spacecraft were being developed and operated, the three-man Apollo program had grown in magnitude and complexity and included a command module, a service module, a lunar module, and a giant Saturn V rocket. The spacecraft and launch vehicle towered 110 meters above the launching pad, and weighed some 3 million kilograms. With the Apollo program, the missions and flight plans had become much more ambitious, the hardware had become more refined, the software had become more sophisticated, and ground support equipment also grew in proportion."[7]

If anything, too much success came too quickly. While Soviet space advances put pressure on NASA to speed up Apollo, the program's inflexible schedule created an inevitable moment of truth. The capsule that showed up at the Kennedy Space Center launch pad possessed more than 19 pounds of combustible materials, and in the wake of the Apollo 1 disaster, the struggle to build Apollo obviously took its toll on the engineers and mechanics. In fact, it ended with the abandonment of Launching pad 34 and a plaque: "Ad Astra per aspera" ("A rough path leads to the stars".

NASA went back to work on Apollo, knowing the Soviets would seize on the opportunity. Apollo 2 and 3 were cancelled, with their objectives segmented into other missions along with the Saturn V rocket.

Apollo 4, 5 and 6 were launched without crews, and when this was judged satisfactory, Apollo had its first flight crews. NASA could replace rockets, but it had a harder time to replace well-trained astronauts, the best pilots America possessed, even if they understood the "rough path" to the "stars" and heeded the words of Grissom: "If we die, we want people to accept it. We hope that is anything happens to us it will not delay the program. This conquest of space is worth the risk of life."[8]

Still, the space program could ill afford to lose any more astronauts during training; and this is exactly what nearly occurred to Armstrong in his preparations for piloting the LEM. As early as 1960, NASA had planned for the proper simulator to train astronauts to land on the Moon, and after many ambitious proposals, NASA settled on the most complex of them all, the Lunar Landing Research Vehicle, a truss of lightweight aluminum mounted to a jet engine. There was a special mode called the lunar simulation mode that the pilot would engage, and the mode commanded the jet engine to support only five-sixths of the LLRV's weight. Along with this, it

---

[7] *The Apollo Spacecraft - A Chronology*, Volume III, "Forward," Newkirk, Roland W, Courtney G. Brooks, and Ivan D. Ertel, January 21, 1966 - July 13, 1974, (NASA SP-4009, 1978), http://www.hq.nasa.gov/office/pao/History/SP-4009/frwrd4.htm

[8] *Rocket Men*, 190.

had a cockpit that rotated freely of the engine so the effect of lunar gravity could then be achieved. A pilot would sit in an open air cockpit, ascend like a plane, and then adjust the jets to behave as they would in lunar gravity. The pilot would then attempt to settle the craft down onto the ground, using the same controls of the LEM.

By 1968, Neil Armstrong and Pete Conrad were in line to command the first lunar missions. Their training took place at Dryden; and Armstrong and Conrad had made 20 and 13 flights respectively. For Armstrong's 21st test flight, the switch into lunar mode went off perfectly until the LLRV went sideways. Armstrong now flew the simulator on his side, and he attempted to right the trainer, but it failed to respond to his controls. The LLRV began to lose altitude rapidly, and Armstrong was left with little recourse but to eject. He did, floating away on a parachute just 200 feet off the ground as the LLRV crashed nearby and erupted into a fireball. Armstrong's only remark to his fellow astronauts was, "I had to bail out of the darn thing."[9] Five of the seven LLRVs ultimately crashed or blew up in flight, but no pilots died.

---

[9] "Apollo LLRV," Encyclopedia Astronautica, http://www.astronautix.com/craft/apoollrv.htm; "When Landing on the Moon, Practice Makes Perfect," http://news.discovery.com/space/history-of-space/when-landing-on-the-moon-practice-makes-perfect-120719.htm

An LLRV

What Armstrong took from that experience is worth mentioning because his skills, more than anything, justified his command of Apollo 11, and ultimately, his role as the first man to step on the Moon. Other factors have been considered for his choice as well: the military chain of command perspective, which favored Armstrong due to NASA's "naval genetic code"; an engineering perspective, with the LEM's design giving precedence to the command pilot who was closer to the door; and lastly, and the personality perspective, which most astronauts identified as Aldrin's "lack of finesse". But above all, Armstrong served as the logical choice due to the abilities he demonstrated as a pilot.[10] During test flights, he had demonstrated the best

---

[10] *Rocket Men*, 19.

qualities of an astronaut-engineer, one who could successfully lead a mission of the Apollo spacecraft and personally set foot on the lunar surface. Apollo was the epitome of technology and training, and Armstrong had all the characteristics of an individual best suited to command a mission from the Earth to the Moon, and most importantly, make the first manned landing.

The ambitiousness of the Saturn-Apollo schedule had cost it the lives of three astronauts, but with the resumption of the missions, NASA seemed back on track. However, the agency and the manned lunar program needed a significant morale boost that ambitions alone could not provide. While "Apollo Applications" provided a blueprint for the future -- lunar bases from used Saturn upper stages, LEM "trucks," and a Venus flyby mission -- the mid-1960s saw the U.S. and the Soviets in nearly the same position. Both seemed ready to launch missions to the Moon.

The U.S.S.R. had achieved a bunch of successes that gave America's space rival the ability to keep pace with the U.S. The soft-landing of the moon probe Luna 9 gave NASA great worry, as too did the rendezvous docking between Soyuz 1 and 2. With that, the Soviets appeared to have two important parts of a mission covered: lunar landing and orbital docking. Soon came the launching of Zond, a further modification of the Soyuz and a worthy rival to Apollo. The Zond was a spacecraft that, while in automated form, could theoretically make the trip to the Moon. The Soviets also stepped up their program with the launch of the LK Lunar Lander, and its impressive orbital maneuvers were later bookended by the other Soviet improvements to Soyuz, with another docking between missions 4 and 5. The Soviets had their moon craft and the ability to land. All they needed was a powerful enough booster, and one that was reliable.[11]

---

[11] "The Soviet Manned Lunar Program," ed. Marcus Lindroos, http://www.fas.org/spp/eprint/lindroos_moon1.htm; "LEK Lunar Expeditionary Complex," Encyclopedia Astronautica, http://astronautix.com/craft/lekmplex.htm; *Rocket Men*, 191, 195, 203.

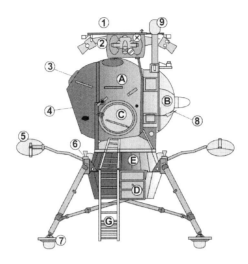

The Soviet design

The success of the Saturn-Apollo complex can be attributed to the original vision of NASA and the first professionals who guided the agency and its plans for spaceflight. More was needed than a reliable rocket; any lunar mission required the best computer and software to navigate and operate the spacecraft. The civilian contribution to U.S. spaceflight, despite its military leanings, began partly from a utopian vision for any type of "Space Race" between nations. Superpowers could compete with one another. As aerospace technologist Paul Lowman says of the success of Apollo, "It seems safe to suggest that his demonstration is a real contribution to prevention of a global thermonuclear war no potential aggressor could plan a surprise attack on the United States without taking into account the military strength implied by it."[12] In a sense, the Space Race kept the Cold War from heating up.

While the professionals who built, tested and launched the Saturn-Apollo complex of ships bore out the tough work of the engineering and mechanical corps of America, their dedication reflected the passion of one of manned spacecraft's founders: Wernher Von Braun, the expatriate rocket scientist from the defeated Third Reich. His military origin notwithstanding, von Braun was repeatedly stymied by U.S. military leaders, even though he did actively court them by touting the benefits of manned spaceflight. Rejected, he offered his vision to the American public, who eagerly read his vision in *Collier's* magazine as early as 1952. With visions of winged rockets and space stations in the public's head, von Braun found it easy to outline a "new" Manhattan Project, one that NASA would eventually adopt, and a blueprint that NASA

---

[12] *Rocket Men*, 91.

would use to court the public sector. No other place demonstrated this early collaboration of civilian and military rocket scientists than Huntsville, Alabama, known also as "Rocket City." Here the first non-military rocket professionals worked on the first rockets to carry Americans into outer space, and a government-funded and civilian-led space program began.[13]

NASA's use of civilian contractors hired by the government created an initial problem that was never properly fixed by the time of Apollo. The agency never had enough experience, which meant that any astronauts who strapped themselves into a capsule on top of a Saturn rocket were in the hands of professionals who were forced to invent spacecraft systems. Despite the gap in experience, the civilian engineers responded with specific knowledge in unproven fields, most notably their invention of escape systems for astronauts in the event of a launch pad accident.[14] After Apollo 1, Nelson explained, "Pad catastrophe was such a grave responsibility, in fact, that NASA had engineered a number of methods to rescue its crews. The key system was a three rocket apparatus -- the launch escape tower -- attached to *Columbia's* [Apollo 11's SC] nose cone, ready to fire, pull the men from their booster, deploy the chutes, and drift into an Atlantic splashdown.[15]

While the engineers and technicians found themselves in tight situations to design launch systems, the Apollo astronauts themselves found themselves increasingly stressed by the pervasive doubts about the quality and duration of their training. "Apollo 11's Neil Armstrong, Buzz Aldrin, and Michael Collins did not themselves feel adequately trained. But they were afraid to admit this to [Deke] Slayton [flight crew operations director]. 'Neil used to come home with his face drawn white, and I was worried about him,' Armstrong's wife, Jan, remembered. 'I was worried about all of them. The worst period was in early June. Their morale was down. They were worried about whether there was time enough for them to learn the things they had to learn, to do the things they had to do, if this mission was to work.'[16]

At the same time, NASA had to deal with requesting funding from a Congress that remembered the early rocket disasters and responded to the space agency's request for money with a modest budget to fund the Saturn rocket. The perception of the civilians who worked on Saturn and Apollo was that their own government prevented them from the creation of an adequate program that could challenge the Soviets and beat them to the Moon.[17] Ultimately, computers made a significant difference in the Apollo Program's success by boosting American confidence in the ability of astronauts to pilot a craft to orbit, land, and return from the Moon. The *Columbia* command module possessed two 17.5-pound Raytheon computers, and the lunar module *Eagle* had one computer. The memory of each one was 36K. While far less impressive

---

[13] Rocket Men, 109, 112.

[14] *Rocket Men*, 145.

[15] *Rocket Men*, 7.

[16] *Rocket Men*, 13.

[17] *Rocket Men*, 150.

than early 21st century cell phones, each computer was much more spectacular in its function, and especially its importance. Nothing was more vital to a mission to the Moon than the computer system with the responsibility to chart the course and deliver the spacecraft to the intended target. This was Guidance and Navigation, which was tasked with guiding the Apollo spacecraft across 250,000 miles of space, orbit around the Moon, land at a targeted location on the surface, guide the *Eagle* from the surface back to the *Columbia* in orbit, guide the *Columbia* towards a space in the Earth's atmosphere that would "capture" the capsule; and land the *Columbia* near a recovery ship in the Pacific Ocean. As Nelson put it in *Rocket Men*, "G&N consisted of a miniature computer with an incredible amount of information in its memory; an array of gyroscopes and accelerometers called the inertial-measurement unit; and a space sextant to enable the navigator to make star sightings. Together they determined precisely the spacecraft location between Earth and Moon, and how best to burn the engines to correct the ship's course or to land at the right spot on the Moon with a minimum expenditure of fuel."[18]

Computers were, in many regards, the key to Apollo 11 solving the key problem of the mission: a circular lunar orbit needed for insertion. How well the astronauts worked with the G&N would leave them with a decision on the far side of the Moon. Either they could use the systems to correct their path to enter orbit, or they would have to burn engines to abort the mission and return home.[19] At least in that scenario, the lives of the astronauts would be saved by the computers, while the tough decision to land or not would be avoided by the cool calculation of a computer.

[18] *Rocket Men*, 220-221.
[19] *Rocket Men*, 225.

The display and keyboard of the Apollo Guidance Computer on the *Columbia*

The helpful advice of a computer might not always be heeded though. During computer simulations of a mission, Armstrong and ground control repeatedly had heated discussions over the possibility of abort, especially if Earth-based radar perceived a threat to landing. In this case, Armstrong refused to defer to computers and rely on his own intuition, which worried NASA mission controllers. They were fearful that a pilot like Armstrong would decide to make a decision that computer simulations said he could not survive, and further ignore the advice of the computers in Houston.[20] NASA was so worried about the possibilities that President Nixon prepared a speech for the event of Apollo 11's crash or inability to leave the Moon.[21] Nixon's statement read:

> "Fate has ordained that the men who went to the moon to explore in peace will stay on the moon to rest in peace. These brave men, Neil Armstrong and Edwin Aldrin, know that there is no hope for their recovery. But they also know that

---

[20] *Rocket Men*, 65.
[21] *Rocket Men*, 69.

there is hope for mankind in their sacrifice. These two men are laying down their lives in mankind's most noble goal: the search for truth and understanding. They will be mourned by their families and friends; they will be mourned by their nation; they will be mourned by the people of the world; they will be mourned by a Mother Earth that dared send two of her sons into the unknown. In their exploration, they stirred the people of the world to feel as one; in their sacrifice, they bind more tightly the brotherhood of man. In ancient days, men looked at stars and saw their heroes in the constellations. In modern times, we do much the same, but our heroes are epic men of flesh and blood. Others will follow and surely find their way home. Man's search will not be denied. But these men were the first, and they will remain the foremost in our hearts. For every human being who looks up at the moon in the nights to come will know that there is some corner of another world that is forever mankind."[22]

Chapter 11: The Apollo 11 Crew

Assembling the crews for Apollo together, and especially the men who would land on the Moon, required combining talents and individuals who could fulfill every complex task along the way. The U.S. space program had begun with military test pilots who became astronauts, and training the astronauts for a lunar mission continued the same grueling tasks.[23] Nelson wrote in *Rocket Men*, "Overtraining' barely described Apollo 11's punishing workload. besides all the astronauts spending fourteen-hour days in the Houston simulators learning everything that could possibly go wrong with machines and their ground controllers, Collins also had a docking simulator at Langley, Virginia, to fly; space suits in Delaware to test; and 10 gs of centrifuge to overcome...Each would-be astronaut was monitored by doctors who tested his response to the stress of ahd decelerations and up to 15 gs of force, pressure that flattened eyeballs and burst capillaries."[24]

Other factors that Apollo astronauts shared with their predecessors were educational and professional backgrounds in engineering.[25] NASA had meant to train astronauts for every single contingency the mission might face, and every astronaut who would go to the Moon also engineered some part of the hardware. Astronauts took part in the process of designing, building, and testing every part of Apollo machinery, meaning each astronaut was an expert, more or less, at some aspect of spaceflight.[26] On Apollo 11, each astronaut personally played a role in the first mission to land a person on the Moon, and they were instrumental in the technical plans of a

---

[22] "Read the Speech Nixon Prepared in Case the Apollo 11 Astronauts Died on the Moon," http://io9.com/5880226/read-the-speech-nixon-prepared-in-case-the-apollo-11-astronauts-died-on-the-moon

[23] *Rocket Men*, 33.

[24] Rocket Men, 59.

[25] *Rocket Men*, 35.

[26] *Rocket Men*, 30.

lunar landing. They had proved to be the best in their field.

Edwin Eugene Aldrin, Jr, (b. January 20, 1930) known by most as Buzz Aldrin, represented the solution that NASA used to face the challenges of a lunar mission. His choice as an astronaut for a Moon mission was more about his technical contributions to the young field of astronautics, and he was very much a military man. Aldrin graduated from West Point in 1951, flew combat missions in F-86s during the Korean War, and worked with more jet fighters for the U.S. Air Force. But ultimately, it was with his Bachelors in Science in Mechanical Engineering, and later, his doctorate in Astronautics from the Massachusetts Institute of Technology, that NASA needed. While NASA rejected Aldrin's application for the astronaut corps when he applied for the Gemini program, his dissertation, "Line-of-sight guidance techniques for manned orbital rendezvous", demonstrated to NASA that Aldrin had the intellectual vision to be an astronaut.[27] He was, after all, the first to ever receive a doctorate in astronautics. This proved enough for the complicated task of a lunar landing. Despite never being a test pilot, Aldrin was chosen as part of the Third Astronaut Class.[28] Aldrin's dissertation also demonstrated his passion, as the dedication of his thesis in January 1963, put it: "In the hopes that this work may in some way contribute to their exploration of space, this is dedicated to the crew members of this country's present and future manned space programs. If only I could join them in their exciting endeavors!"

---

[27] Line of sight guidance techniques for manned orbital rendezvous
[28] http://www.jsc.nasa.gov/Bios/htmlbios/aldrin-b.html

Aldrin

   The inclusion of Aldrin in the astronaut corps signaled a new direction for NASA's planning. While NASA had included engineers before, key among them Gus Grissom, the inclusion of Aldrin into the corps was a recognition of the giant leap NASA must undertake to make a Moon landing successful. At this point, the American space agency was undecided on the plan to reach the Moon. Would it be an Earth Orbit Rendezvous between spacecraft, or would it take place in Lunar Orbit? In 1963, NASA could have gone either way, and even Direct Ascent was not out of the picture yet. NASA realized they had not pulled off any orbital rendezvous at all between spacecraft, and Aldrin was picked in order to make the docking between craft a very real possibility, regardless of the location of the rendezvous.

Aldrin discovered during the writing of his astronautical thesis something he called the "orbital paradox", and his discovery proved to be a formative step in the direction of a successful moon mission: "If you're trying to pilot your orbiting spaceship to reach a spaceship in a higher orbit, the intuitive course is to (1) aim your spacecraft up, towards the higher orbit, and (2) speed up your spacecraft so it will catch up. Dr. Aldrin describes the surprising result of this maneuver. You'll 'end up in an even higher orbit, traveling at a slower speed and watching the second craft fly off into the distance.'"[29]

Aldrin's genius was coming up with a way to train astronauts to dock with a spacecraft using direct observation of the target vehicle. This line-of-sight method would not be done alone; the pilot would use their direct visuals to complement and augment the computers on board the spaceship. Navigation would be a two-part act between man and machine, but Aldrin felt the combination not only made orbital rendezvous easier but also allowed astronauts to actually pilot the craft. Aldrin intended to train astronauts to ignore their "intuitions as fighter pilots" in space, "a world of three dimensions" where "there was no up and down." They should be able to manually fly their craft and dock with another during a Moon mission, even in an emergency without help from a computer.

Aldrin's intent to train an astronaut to manually fly the craft was more in line with the endless disagreements between the engineers and the astronauts. "There will forever be disagreements over who, exactly, flies NASA ships -- the engineers on the ground, or the spacemen in the capsules. Later in life, as most of his colleagues continued to claim the pilot role, Aldrin sided with the engineers: 'Gemini and Apollo were computerized and pre-planned, so the era of the pilot in command, having the creativity to decide what he wants to do -- that's gone. Only in an emergency is it apparent. And in an emergency, like Apollo 13, they had no idea what went wrong. It was like, 'We have a problem, all the lights are comin' on!' And it was up to the ground to figure out what the problem was'"[30]

If Aldrin appeared to side with the engineers, he didn't have the chance to act like one during Gemini 12, when he and James Lovell launched into space on a 4-day mission in 1966. In addition to performing a 5 ½ hour spacewalk, necessary for any moon mission that involved two spacecraft, Aldrin was forced to manually dock the Gemini spacecraft with the Agena docking vehicle.[31] Without the targeting, it was left up to Aldrin to perform what he had originally designed: the successful training of an astronaut to pilot a craft in conjunction with a computer and navigational charts. Aldrin, in a sense, stood somewhere between the engineers and the astronauts, both of whom "honored" his obsession with orbital rendezvous with the moniker "Dr. Rendezvous."[32] Nelson noted, "As an astronaut, Aldrin revealed both his smarts and his

[29] Dr. Buzz Aldrin and the Orbital Rendezvous
[30] Rocket Men, 243.
[31] NASA, Biographical Data, "Edwin Buzz Aldrin", http://www.jsc.nasa.gov/Bios/htmlbios/aldrin-b.html
[32] "Dr. Buzz Aldrin and the Orbital Paradox," http://tranquilitybaseblog.blogspot.com/2012/12/dr-buzz-aldrin-and-

simultaneous lack thereof in promulgating his MIT studies so assiduously and his opinions so stubbornly that it annoyed many of his colleagues. 'His doctoral thesis on space rendezvous...made him, in his own eyes, one of the world's leading experts,' flight director Chris Kraft said. 'Before long, the real experts...were calling him, with a touch of sarcasm, 'Dr. Rendezvous.'"[33]

Ironically, Aldrin's authorship of orbiting rendezvous would make the Gemini Program successful. Gemini has long been considered a mixed bag, but it did what it had to do. First and foremost, it showed that orbital docking between two craft could be achieved, or at the very least, it showed the U.S. could achieve this feat (the Soviets had also proved to be successful at this space endeavor). Second, it settled once and for all that orbital rendezvous, at least in Earth orbit, could be attempted and completed. By orbiting around the Earth, Gemini almost accomplished something that had never been intended; it very nearly made the Apollo Program and the idea of LOR redundant. For a brief time, the idea of EOR seemed to work just fine, and at one point Gemini was seen as the craft to get Americans to the Moon first.

Gemini was referred to as "Mercury Mark II" upon inception, but the program always had an initial identity that differentiated the spacecraft from Mercury. From the beginning, James Chamberlin and the manufacturer of Gemini, McDonnell Aircraft, considered Gemini as a viable option and competitor to the Apollo program that could accomplish a Moon landing at just 5% of the cost. They also thought Gemini could get men to the moon by 1966. Gemini would take advantage of the work on the Saturn (C) rocket, which in early 1960 was seen as one part of the larger vehicle for a Direct Ascent. Gemini took life as a docking craft, and then it evolved into a fleet of craft to dock with "trans-stage target vehicles" (upper stage Centaur rockets) to accomplish lunar flybys.

Eventually, Chamberlin attempted to combine Gemini with the Apollo program in order to take advantage of the successes with the Saturn rocket. Gemini II was always billed as a possible Direct Ascent craft that could land on the Moon as a capsule with retrograde stage, upper stage ascent module, and foldable landing legs. The options to use different modules with "advanced" Gemini envisioned a fleet of craft -- "Big Gemini" -- that could rendezvous with space stations, ferry passengers from low to high orbits, and even provide a lifeboat and rescue craft for Moon explorers. To Chamberlin and McDonnell Aircraft, Gemini was the modular craft that NASA could use for years to stake a hold in Earth orbit and on the surface of the Moon.[34]

Gemini's potential never overcame the vision that Apollo encapsulated in a design that allowed the engineers to develop visionary craft to undertake LOR -- which NASA grew increasingly

---

orbital-paradox.html
[33] *Rocket Men*, 46.
[34] "By Gemini to the Moon," http://www.astronautix.com/articles/bygemoon.htm ; "Gemini on the Moon," http://www.wired.com/wiredscience/2012/05/gemini-on-the-moon-1962/

fond of -- and work with a large booster, the Saturn V (C-5) that promised to launch even more ambitious spacecraft than Gemini could. As a government project, the Apollo program was unrivaled and even considered a logical successor to the Manhattan Project, with the engineering and government assisted programs and agencies the program created and supported over the decade.[35] As Nelson put it in *Rocket Men*, "In so many ways, the race to the Moon would turn out to be a sequel to its predecessor's race for atomic mastery. Bother were enormous projects that only a great nation, on a federal level, could afford to attempt, and achieve. Both began with Third Reich émigrés, and a shared geography [New Mexico]."[36]

With the view of Gemini as mostly a "trainer" for U.S. astronauts, the narrative of men who traveled to the Moon makes sense and, upon first impression, follows a logical pattern. From the years 1965-1966, nine successive launches took place, and every Apollo astronaut rode on a Gemini spacecraft and participated in an ambitious schedule of experiments, maneuvers, and assessment of technology. During this time, EOR was the "cradle" for the plan to rendezvous two craft in space, and Gemini's astronauts took part in those missions. The program had started as a spacecraft designed to take advantage of the lessons from the Mercury Program, but also, and quite purposely, being built by astronauts with higher degrees in mechanical and aeronautical engineering. As each of Gemini's names represented the different intentions behind the program, such as "Mercury Mark II" meant to suggest its replacement of the first space capsule, the name "Gus Mobile" informed people in joking terms that Virgil Ivan Grissom, better known as Gus Grissom, had designed the spacecraft for astronauts to be more than passengers. Gemini taught astronauts how to *fly* in Earth-orbit.[37]

Neil A. Armstrong (August 5, 1930 – August 25, 2012) got his bachelor's degree in aeronautical engineering and master's in aerospace engineering, which gave him the solid foundation he would need to contribute to the U.S. space program. He did so immediately by joining the National Advisory Council for Aeronautics (NACA) from 1949-1952.[38] He took the knowledge he gained as a naval aviator to NASA's "High Speed Flight Station." In the spot that was to become the Dryden Flight Research Station, Armstrong flew 200 models of experimental aircraft over the Mojave Desert, including jets, rockets, helicopters, and gliders. He even test piloted the 4000 mph X-15 and the Dyna-Soar, the Air Force's attempt at a winged suborbital spacecraft.[39] Armstrong explained, "I did a lot of different test programs in those days. That was the first time I ever flew supersonic. We had two B-29s that were sued for dropping rocket aircraft, the X-1s and the Skyrockets. So I, either as the right-seat or the left-seat guy in the B-29, launched over one hundred rocket airplanes in the fifties."[40]

---

[35] *Rocket Men*, 36.

[36] *Rocket Men*, 36.

[37] "Gemini: 1965-1966," http://www.spacecollection.info/us_gemini/gemini.html;

[38] "Neil A. Armstrong," Biographical Data, http://www.jsc.nasa.gov/Bios/htmlbios/armstrong-na.html

[39] "Farewell Neil Armstrong: The Ultimate Test Pilot," http://www.wired.com/wiredscience/2012/08/neil-armstrong_test-pilot/

Neil Armstrong

    While fellow astronauts would later comment that Armstrong was viewed as the "weakest" on the "[steering] stick," Armstrong came to the astronaut corps in 1962 with multiple levels of experience. His flight-time with diverse craft not only allowed him to handle different engineering characteristics but also gave him moments to work through unexpected malfunctions and other non-operable problems. "Inside the small world of military aviation, his exploits as a test pilot are still spoken of with awe. One of the stories that is told is that after landing a plane in the desert after its engines had both failed, Armstrong was rolling to a stop when he saw an obstacle that he was about to crash into. According to the legend, he used his speed and the flaps and rudders of his aircraft to force the plane up onto one wheel and, like a movie stunt driver, swerved around the obstacle precariously balanced on a single bit of rubber."[41]

---

[40] *Rocket Men*, 51.

[41] "Buzz Aldrin: Neil Armstrong Was the 'Best Pilot I Ever Knew,"
http://www.thedailybeast.com/articles/2012/08/27/buzz-aldrin-neil-armstrong-was-the-best-pilot-i-ever-knew.html

Mechanical challenges forced Armstrong to think quick, make rapid decisions, and possess the coolness and acumen to take control of an aircraft. His colleagues recognized his skills in those regards quickly.[42] After Armstrong's death in 2012, Buzz Aldrin called him the "best pilot I ever knew." An article in *The Daily Beast* noted, "His skill as a research and test pilot certainly impressed Buzz Aldrin...Aldrin said in an interview with The Daily Beast shortly after his former colleague's death. That is high praise indeed coming from a man who had flown F-86 jet fighters in combat in Korea and who has his own impressive set of flying and technical academic credentials. Armstrong's ability to memorize the smallest engineering detail and to be able to explain, in even more detail, the intricate working of any aircraft he tested made him the outstanding test pilot of his generation. To this day, within military aviation, he is famous for his "steel trap" mind and his unflappable demeanor."[43]

After his arrival with the second class of NASA astronauts, Armstrong flew on Gemini VIII in 1966 as the command pilot. It would be Gemini's sixth manned flight, but the first to dock two spacecraft. Along with his pilot, David R. Scott, Armstrong would dock the Gemini capsule with a Gemini Agena Target Vehicle (GATV). The launch of both spacecraft went flawlessly, and the docking commenced without a hitch. Aided by computers and navigation software, as well as Aldrin's "training for orbital rendezvous", Armstrong was the first astronaut to pilot a craft and dock it with another spacecraft.

For 27 minutes, the mission proceeded as planned. Scott prepared for a two hour spacewalk, partly in preparation for expectation of EOR and the training for a lunar mission. Suddenly, both spacecraft began to tumble wildly and out of control. Armstrong immediately detached from the GATV, but the tumbling continued and then intensified. Gemini VIII was out of control.[44] An article in *Discovery* described the situation:

> "The men in Houston got confirmation that the spacecraft had separated just as Armstrong pulled the Gemini back and Scott hit the undock switch. Unfortunately, the separation didn't help the astronauts. Scott called down as calmly as he could, 'We have serious problems here. We're– we're tumbling end over end up here. We're disengaged from the Agena.' They tried to explain to mission control what was happening. 'We're rolling up and we can't turn anything off,' Armstrong said. 'Continuously increasing in a left roll.' Armstrong fought without success to dampen out the spacecraft's tumbling. Turning things over to Scott didn't help; he was equally unsuccessful. By then, Gemini 8 was making one full revolution *per second*. The centrifugal force building up inside the spacecraft was making loose items — flight plants, checklists, and procedure charts —

[42] "From the Mojave to the Moon: Neil Armstrong's Early NASA Years,"
http://www.nasa.gov/missions/research/neil_armstrong.html
[43] "Buzz Aldrin: Neil Armstrong Was the 'Best Pilot I Ever Knew,"
http://www.thedailybeast.com/articles/2012/08/27/buzz-aldrin-neil-armstrong-was-the-best-pilot-i-ever-knew.html;
[44] "Gemini 8," National Space Science Data Center, http://nssdc.gsfc.nasa.gov/nmc/spacecraftDisplay.do?id=1966-020A;

stick to the walls. Their heads and arms were pinned against the backs of their seats making reaching the hand controllers an effort. The sunlight coming in through the windows was flashing as fast as a strobe light.[45]

Gemini VIII

The only thing Armstrong could do was end the flight and begin re-entry, since the alternative of Scott and him struck by a blackout would have doomed them. He reached back behind his seat and felt for the re-entry control system. Once engaged, the spacecraft stopped its tumble, and Scott fed line code into the computer to program new re-entry information. Gemini splashed down on Earth, and the investigation began. It turned out one of Gemini's eight control thrusters had been stuck in the on-position. When it fired thrust repeatedly, the spacecraft had responded by tumbling, but the crew of Gemini VIII had survived through their grasp of the situation and the creation of a solution to save the capsule. Armstrong's training as a pilot proved to be the most crucial factor. By avoiding a catastrophe, Armstrong had also kept NASA on track with its projected mission schedule for the Moon.[46]

---

[45] "The Vomit-inducing Gemini 8 Mission," http://news.discovery.com/space/history-of-space/neil-armstrong-at-the-helm-120730.htm

[46] "The Vomit-inducing Gemini 8 Mission," http://news.discovery.com/space/history-of-space/neil-armstrong-at-

Chapter 12: Finishing Touches

A great deal of anxiety surrounded NASA about the quality of the rockets and spaceships, the training of the ground crews and astronauts, and the coordination between humans and computers. For Apollo, disaster was much closer to reality than anyone wanted to admit. Already, tragedy had struck the program during Apollo 1.

Two things happened that put Apollo on course to land on the Moon. The first was Apollo 8, the first all-up mission of a Saturn V and a crewed ship towards the Moon. Understandably, most people can name Apollo 11 as the first mission to land men on the Moon, and a critically acclaimed film about Apollo 13's harrowing mission was released in 1995, but this has also meant that the rest of the Apollo missions have been greatly overshadowed, including Apollo 8, despite the fact Apollo 8 accomplished several firsts and ultimately made Apollo 11 possible.

NASA launched Apollo 7 on October 11, 1968. Apollo 7 was a manned mission that tested the command/service modules in Earth's orbit and reentry. The successful mission demonstrated the viability of the command/service module to enter Earth's orbit and survive reentry back into the Earth's atmosphere. Apollo 8 was originally intended to test the lunar module in orbit and reentry, as Apollo 7 had done for the command/service module, but in June 1968, NASA suffered a setback with the lunar modules, which compromised the planned December 1968 date for Apollo 8's launch.

Since the lunar modules weren't ready, and the command/service modules had already been successfully tested in Earth's orbit and reentry, NASA decided in August to change Apollo 8's mission, making it a manned mission to orbit around the Moon in the command/service module. This would allow NASA to test the command/service module's lunar orbit procedures, and, of course, score a huge propaganda victory in the Space Race.

On December 21, 1968, Apollo 8 was launched by a Saturn V rocket. All three stages of the Saturn V rocket had been tested in previous launches, including the crucial third stage that had to reactivate to accelerate the spacecraft out of Earth's orbit and toward the Moon. The previous unmanned mission suffered a failure of the third stage's Trans Lunar Injection sequence, but the Saturn V carrying Apollo 8 worked almost perfectly. About three hours after launching, the Apollo 8 crew became the first humans to escape Earth's orbit and take pictures of the entire planet as a whole.

Apollo 8 cruised toward the Moon for nearly three whole days before it was time for the Lunar Orbit Insertion. Four minutes later, the crew became the first humans to enter the Moon's orbit and see the far side of the Moon in person. While orbiting, the crew reconnoitered the Moon's surface, eventually describing the "Sea of Tranquility" well enough that it would become Apollo

11's planned landing site.

As Apollo 8 continued orbiting around the Moon, it witnessed the Earth rising and snapped the iconic "Earthrise" photo of the globe from the Moon's vantage point on December 24. On Christmas Day, after several orbits around the Moon and the first ever live broadcast interview from the Moon's orbit, Apollo 8 prepared to head home.

On the voyage home, crewmember Jim Lovell inadvertently switched off certain navigational readings for the module's computers. This accident required using the module's thrusters to manually realign the spacecraft for reentry. The mistake was quickly corrected, but it fortuitously gave Lovell the experience to do it for Apollo 13 under more trying circumstances.

On the afternoon of December 27, 1968, Apollo 8 splashed down safely in the Pacific Ocean. In addition to setting history, the three crewmembers, Lovell, Frank Borman and William Anders, were named Time's Men of the Year.

The success of a mission that orbited the Moon and returned home reinvigorated NASA and the Apollo Program. The success of the mission proved what many at NASA had said for a year. Saturn could launch men to the Moon; and the Soviets and their N-1 booster -- it continued to explode on the launch pad or fall back to the Earth. It seemed the U.S. had the space it needed to beat the Soviets.[47] All that was left was to launch and pilot Apollo 11.

---

[47] *Rocket Men*, 195.

Picture of Earth taken by Apollo 8

Apollo 8's success had also benefited its backup crew, which included Neil Armstrong and Buzz Aldrin. Neil Armstrong later explained:

> "We were very excited about [Apollo 8]...We thought it was very bold, because we still had the problem on the Saturn and we'd had a couple problems with [both] Saturn V launches, so to take the next one, and without those problems being demonstrated as solved, and put men, a crew on it, not just take it into orbit, to take it to the Moon, it seemed incredibly aggressive. But we were for it. We thought that was a wonderful opportunity. If we could make it work, why, it would make us a giant leap ahead. It showed a lot of courage on the part of NASA

management to make that step. One of the things I was concerned with at the time was whether our navigation was sufficiently accurate, that we could, in fact, devise a trajectory that would get us around the Moon at the right distance without, say, hitting the Moon on the back side of something like that, and if we lost communication with Earth, for whatever reason, could we navigate by ourselves using celestial navigation. We thought we could, but these were undemonstrated skills."[48]

The Gemini program prepared to conclude its original mission objective as a trainer of Apollo astronauts in the year 1966, and the 10th mission rocketed into space carrying astronauts Michael Collins and John W. Young. They had a full mission in front of them, charged with the accomplishment of former Gemini objectives left unfulfilled by the cancellation of missions. Collins and Young's flight had big ramifications that made Apollo 8 successful, including the ability to dock with an Agena module, fire the module's rockets, achieve a higher orbit to rendezvous with another Agena module (one that was derelict and without radar) and perform a space walk over to the module. Every step that Gemini X achieved gave NASA the confidence that Apollo 8's lunar flyby could be completed. So successful was Gemini X that NASA would give Collins the responsibility as the command/service module (CSM) pilot on Apollo 8.

[48] *Rocket Men*, 198.

Michael Collins

An emergency back surgery took Collins off the mission and nearly ended his astronaut career, but his recovery allowed NASA to put him back won the Apollo Program and on the next available mission for the Moon. With Apollo 10's successful mock-up and rehearsal for the Moon landing in lunar orbit, NASA could put Collins in the pilot seat of the CSM *Columbia* on Apollo 11.[49]

Michael Collins (b. October 31, 1930) was a rarity among NASA astronauts. He was a United States Air Forces test pilot, far different than the greater pool of pilots NASA recruited from, which typically included aviators from the Navy and Marine Corps. His 5,000 hours spent in the air gave him excellent control of the "stick," which led to his inclusion in the Astronaut Group Three of 1963 and made him one of the best pilots in NASA.[50] He was used to carrying out experimental missions and was perfectly comfortable in that capacity. He would be required to

[49] "Gemini X (10)," http://nssdc.gsfc.nasa.gov/nmc/masterCatalog.do?sc=1966-066A
[50] "Biographical Data (Michael Collins")," http://www.jsc.nasa.gov/Bios/htmlbios/collins-m.html; "Astronaut Group Three," http://grin.hq.nasa.gov/ABSTRACTS/GPN-2000-001476.html

accomplish pilot-tasks that no other aviator had ever done, primarily the one thing no Apollo mission could test for: the rendezvous with a lunar module on-return from the Moon with two astronauts onboard. Years later Collins remarked on the test of his skills as an aviator he would most likely be remembered for: "My secret terror for the last six months has been leaving them on the Moon and returning to Earth alone; now I am within minutes of finding out the truth of the matter...If they fail to rise from the surface, or crash back into it, I am not going to commit suicide; I am coming home, forthwith, but I will be a marked man for life and I know it."[51]

A good solution for Collins to avoid the infamy of "stranding" Armstrong and Aldrin on the Moon lay with the Guidance and Navigation system. Computers and navigation software were one part of it, and gyroscopes also helped a pilot keep track of the three-dimensions of outer space; but it was the experience of Collins that made the difference in the success of Apollo. Collins, like the Apollo astronauts before and after him, would wear an eye patch to avoid the fatigue of endless hours of squinting. He peered through the ship's sextant to sight stars in the night sky, no different than navigators had done for hundreds of generations on board sailing ships. When he located the position and altitudes of the stars, he combined the results with the onboard data of the ship's speed and position. The purpose of this was to fire the CSM's rocket and send Apollo 11 on its course to the Moon.[52]

The Guidance and Navigation unit was only as good as its human operator, and that responsibility also lay with Collins. When the gyroscopes were correctly set, Collins was in charge with the dial-in of the position of the two reference stars. The navigation system would then compare the ship's position with the Inertial Measuring Unit, and the thrusters were fired to set the ship on its course. The problem with this, as Apollo 8, 9, and 10 learned, was that the amount of sunlight hitting the spacecraft made it difficult to recognize stars without the surrounding constellations. Collins proved good at using the sextant's computer to find the stars.[53]

Collins' proficiency with the challenges of flight and navigation worked to ease the many problems Apollo faced in landing men on the Moon. For one, serious gaps in knowledge about the Moon's composition challenged NASA, and that serious lack of data could potentially compromise the mission. The Ranger and Surveyor probes had done an excellent job mapping the Moon, but the astronauts had a feeling that, along with their training, there was not enough knowledge of the surface terrain to inform targeted landing sites.[54]

Collins also worried about things out of his control, mainly the technologies that were responsible for landing the LEM *Eagle* on the Moon and the return trip. The LEM's upper stage,

---

[51] "How Michael Collins Became the Forgotten Astronaut of Apollo 11," http://www.guardian.co.uk/science/2009/jul/19/michael-collins-astronaut-apollo11

[52] *Rocket Men*, 220.

[53] *Rocket Men*, 221.

[54] *Rocket Men*, 230.

the vehicle responsible for the delivery of Armstrong and Aldrin from the Moon's surface to the CSM in orbit, had developed an instability. Sometimes during dress-rehearsals, it would not separate from the descent stage. This would have trapped the astronauts on the Moon.[55]

Another issue that developed belonged to the contingencies of things the engineers at NASA could not plan for and would only know at the moment of truth, when the *Eagle* was on its way to the lunar surface. Engineers questioned whether imaging radar would work on the LEM, and whether or not the data could be simultaneously communicated with the CSM and Mission Control back on Earth.[56] The matter of docking the *Columbia* and *Eagle* also gave NASA fits, as the history of near disasters during rendezvous and space walks had never been completely solved. Most astronauts had gotten sick during EVAs outside of their spaceship, as the strain to maneuver in zero gravity fatigued them. NASA knew in an emergency that EVAs might be all that could save the crew, especially if Armstrong and Aldrin had to move from the LEM to the CSM.[57]

NASA flight managers and Apollo astronauts, aware of all the things that could go wrong, counted on the skill and dedication of professionals like Collins to offset the challenges and dangers that could potentially destroy the mission. His position as the CSM pilot carried a great honor and responsibility. No astronaut could pilot the capsule unless they had done before. At that time in the flight order of Apollo astronauts, none had, so Collins was the only astronaut who NASA felt could be entrusted with the job to circle the Moon alone and await the two astronauts who would descend to the surface and hopefully return. As Armstrong put it:

> "I was certainly aware that this was a culmination of the work of 300,000 or 400,000 people over a decade and that the nation's hopes and outward appearance largely rested on how the results came out...And you know, I have no complaints about the way my colleagues were able to step up to that....when you have hundreds of thousands of people all doing their job a little better than they have to, you get an improvement in performance. And that's the reason we could have pulled this whole thing off...when I was working here at the Manned Spacecraft Center, you could stand across the street and you could not tell when quitting time was, because people didn't leave at quitting time in those days. People just worked, and they worked until whatever their job was [was] done...And whenever you have those ingredients, whether it be government or private industry or a retail store, you're going to win."[58]

---

[55] *Rocket Men*, 12.
[56] *Rocket Men*, 17.
[57] *Rocket Men*, 297.
[58] *Rocket Men*, 81-82.

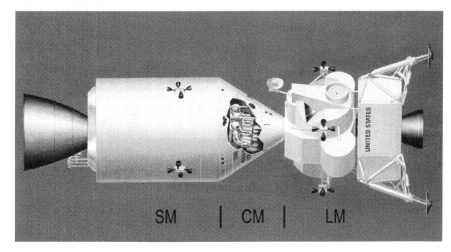

The service module, command module, and lunar module design for Apollo 11

At the end of 1968, the country was celebrating the historic and successful Apollo 8 mission, as was NASA. But NASA also realized that the mission only occurred due to a setback with the lunar module that would actually land on the Moon. In March 1969, the unheralded Apollo 9 tested the lunar module's maneuvers for several days in Earth's orbit before successfully reentering Earth's atmosphere.

By May 1969, NASA was ready to do an entire dry run of landing men on the Moon. Apollo 10 was sent into lunar orbit with the command/service module and lunar module, and on May 22, a lunar module descended toward the Moon for the first time. The lunar module was manned, but the ascent stage was not fully fueled, so it could not complete an entire descent. The automated system worked, and the modules successfully re-docked together. Apollo 10 successfully splashed down on May 26, and with that, NASA was ready to land men on the Moon.

Before Collins could pilot the CSM with attached LEM to the Moon, the Saturn V booster needed to accomplish the most dangerous part of the mission: the launch. The astronauts rode the high-speed elevator 320 feet to the Apollo capsule and strapped into their flight seats. The countdown began at 2 hours and 46 minutes. The Soviets struggled throughout the 1960s to design rockets up to the task, but NASA got it right with the Saturn V rocket, which to this day remains the most powerful launching rocket NASA ever used. The Saturn V rockets were truly gargantuan, standing nearly 350 feet tall and holding thousands of tons of fuel. These rockets could carry a payload weighing over 250,000 pounds into orbit, giving it the ability to launch the

Apollo spacecraft into orbit in about 12 minutes at nearly 18,000 miles per hour. But that was just the beginning of the Saturn V's duties. Once in orbit, the Saturn V still had to accelerate the spacecraft to nearly 25,000 miles per hour to allow the spacecraft to escape the Earth's orbit and head for the Moon.

Designing rocket engines that powerful was hard enough, but NASA had to design the Saturn V to accomplish its duties in multiple stages, because an Apollo spacecraft typically had to spend a few hours in orbit around the Earth before heading for the Moon. Thus, the Saturn V's first two stages would accelerate the spacecraft to about 15,000 miles per hour, while the third and final stage would enter the spacecraft into Earth's orbit at about 18,000 miles per hour. But this third and final stage also had to be capable of essentially restarting and reaccelerating to propel the spacecraft out of Earth's orbit and to the Moon at about 25,000 miles per hour. Not only was Saturn V capable of getting the job done, but it also got the job done successfully every time it was used. NASA relied on Saturn V rockets more than a dozen times without a major accident during the 1960s and 1970s.

With the last adjustments made to leaky hydrogen fuel valves, the five mammoth F-1 engines fired. The rocket lifted, moving slightly -- some astronauts called it a faint 'wobble' -- and the rockets gimbaled slightly to keep everything on course. Nothing held the spaceship upright but the columns of thrust. A launch controller said the words the crew most wanted to hear: the rocket had cleared the tower. Within seconds, Apollo 11 was lifted hundreds of feet into the air and its auto program began a roll. The ship was on course towards the first objective. The first stage of the Saturn V rocket would accelerate the spacecraft to over 6,000 miles per hour in two and a half minutes before detaching and falling away. The second stage accelerated the spacecraft to about 15,000 miles per hour after six more minutes before falling away. If all went well, Apollo 11 would orbit the Earth in a little more than 11 minutes.[59]

---

[59] "Apollo Flight Journey," Apollo 11, Day 1, Part 1: Launch, http://www.hq.nasa.gov/alsj/a11/a11.html

The Launch Control Center before liftoff

After two orbits of the Earth, Collins was commanded by Houston Control to ignite the third stage of the Saturn V, known as the "Translunar Injection". This stage would accelerate the spacecraft to about 25,000 mph to reach the escape velocity necessary to escape Earth's orbit. At this time, the lunar module attached to the service/command module, and once the spacecraft reached escape velocity, the Saturn V's third stage fell away on a different trajectory.

Apollo 11's picture of Earth during the Translunar Injection

The engines fired on and shot Apollo 11 on its course to the Moon, a journey that would take three days of cruising and a short engine burst known as the "Lunar Orbit Insertion" procedure to properly position the spacecraft to be captured by the Moon's orbit. NASA had mapped the Moon during previous missions, in order to help choose the landing sites for the Apollo lunar modules. When the Moon captured the spacecraft, the spacecraft would complete several orbits around the Moon to properly line up the lunar module for descent.

Chapter 14: Traveling to the Moon

As this part of the journey began, Aldrin turned on the color camera inside the capsule, and already viewers on Earth witnessed the historic trip that might or might not land men on the Moon. Of course, one thing the camera could not capture was the mental state inside the capsule. Nelson captured the mood in *Rocket Men* by describing how Collins felt about the other two astronauts:

> "Of the three, Collins was always the 'easy-going guy who brought levity into things,' as Buzz Aldrin recalled. During the run-up to their mission, Collins tried to foster a sense of camaraderie, but could only get so far. After Armstrong's bulwark of shyness proved impenetrable, Collins decided that Neil 'never transmits anything but the surface layer, and that only sparingly. I like him, but I don't know what to make of him, or how to get to know him better.' He doesn't seem willing to meet you halfway...Buzz, on the other hand, is more approachable; in fact, for reasons I cannot fully explain, it is me that seems to be trying to keep him at arm's length. I have the feeling that he would probe me for weaknesses, and that makes me uncomfortable."[60]

Perhaps the astronauts, much to the chagrin of the "easy-going" Collins, were men much more comfortable with their thoughts. The view of the Earth from orbit had already inspired the crew and left them to ponder the "imaginary lines that you can't see."[61] Once on the way to the Moon, though, having left the Earth behind, no reference points existed. Only the blackness of space awaited them; and the spaceship was engulfed by the expanse of dark and the glitter of stars.[62]

All the crew could do at this point was go through their various duties; Collins attended to the tasks of purging fuel cells, dumping wastewater, recharging batteries, and replacing carbon dioxide filters. Armstrong and Aldrin went over procedures to land. They also had to eat. "On Apollo 11, ham, tuna, and chicken salad sandwich spreads were squeezed out of a tube...Freeze dried entrees...of roast beef, ham, potatoes, yam, bacon, applesauce, vegetable medley, and hash were vacuum-sealed in plastic and needed to be rehydrated with three shots of hot water and kneaded into a mush, which was then, again, squeezed out like toothpaste."[63]

Still, the astronauts on Apollo 11 enjoyed the trip, especially the sensation of weightlessness,[64] and Apollo 11 experienced a unique visual phenomenon on the way to the Moon. The further the ship traveled, the harder it became to see the Moon. Collins pitched the ship so the crew could have a view of their destination, but they did not have much time to appreciate the view. On July 19, the fourth day of the mission, they would make the burn of the CSM's single thruster to achieve orbit. This, like other events on the trip, was the moment of truth. Either Apollo 11 would successfully enter the orbit of the Moon in order to land on the surface, or the burn would

---

[60] *Rocket Men*, 43.
[61] *Rocket Men*, 212.
[62] *Rocket Men*, 216.
[63] *Rocket Men*, 217.
[64] *Rocket Men*, 218.

fail and they would have to abort the mission.

NASA soon received the signal from the dark side of the Moon, where Apollo 11 had now entered. They were "go" for lunar orbit. The mission to land on the Moon was still on.[65]

Looking out over the lunar surface, the crew lauded the near-perfect precision of the orbital insertion and compared notes about their perceptions of the Moon's "true" color. NASA asked them to identify the "landing path," and the crew looked for identifying craters, with a sudden panic at the realization that the topography nearly looked identical from one section to the other. Collins and Armstrong eventually made headway of the location of their bearings, but they quickly realized the Moon's true mystery. To the astronauts, the Moon was an "unwelcoming" and "unfriendly" place.[66] Collins later reflected on that moment, "I feel that all of us are aware that the honeymoon is over and we are about to lay our little pink bodies on the line...We have not been able to see the Moon for nearly a day now, and the change is electrifying....The Moon changes character as the angle of sunlight strikes its surface changes....It starts off very forbidding, becomes friendly and then becomes forbidding again as the Sun disappears."[67]

Indeed, Collins was right. The moment came to put their "little pink bodies on the line." After 13 orbits around the Moon, Armstrong and Aldrin dressed in the EVA suits, also known as "white, thirteen-layered, Mylar-and-Teflon-coated beta-cloth Integrated Thermal Meteoroid Garments."[68] Both astronauts took their positions inside the LEM *Eagle*. Collins also had to dress-up in a spacesuit, just in case he needed to make an emergency spacewalk.

To descend thousands of feet down to the Moon's surface, the lunar module had both an engine and thrusters that would allow it to maintain speed, control and direction. The lunar module would descend in a pirouette to help it descend straight, but as Apollo 11's lunar module inadvertently proved, any incorrect timing or ill-timed thrust would land a module several miles away from its intended destination, which could be the difference between a smooth landing or landing among boulders and craters. For most of the descent, the lunar module was automated, but the final stage of the descent required manual controls, and once the descent stage was finished, it would fall away from the module like the Saturn V rocket stages.

[65] *Rocket Men*, 226.
[66] *Rocket Men*, 226.
[67] *Rocket Men*, 227.
[68] *Rocket Men*, 233.

Armstrong and Aldrin did not sit down in the cockpit; they would fly the *Eagle* in an upright position, velcroed and tethered to the walls and floors. The LEM's appearance was function over form, appearing almost like an insect. It had the thinnest of skins, consisting of barely three sheets of aluminum foil. As one engineer explained, "aesthetics be hanged." The bug-eyed lander would accomplish the final vision of NASA's moon mission and land two men on the Moon by operating like a dinghy. The lower descent engine and stage would be left on the surface, and the ascent stage would bring the astronauts back to the *Columbia*, only to be cut loose and left to drift away into space.[69]

Chapter 15: One Small Step for Man

Once Collins blew the explosive bolts, the *Eagle* now operated under its own electrical power. Armstrong swiveled the LEM around, so Collins could check the full deployment of its landing legs. Armstrong, as mission commander, gave the signal, "The Eagle has wings."

---

[69] *Rocket Men*, 234.

Now came the moment no amount of simulation could have anticipated, and the moment NASA and the astronauts feared most of all. No matter the amount of training, fine tunings in orbital calculation and speed were still not as exact as mission planners would have liked. And sure enough, the first problem of the many still to come occurred when the separation between *Columbia* and *Eagle* created more thrust than intended. Along with the mistakes in calculating the gravity of the Moon and its influence on the ships, this ensured the original landing site would be overshot by four miles, setting the *Eagle* on a path towards a field of boulders.[70]

Back on Earth in Houston at Mission Control (MOCR), a sprawling community college-like campus, the situation was closely monitored by an imaginative and dedicated corps of controllers who prided themselves on their ability to solve problems. They now would have one. In front of the 20x10 foot screen showing the two tiny dots that were *Columbia* and *Eagle* flashing slowly across a giant picture of the Moon, the controllers sat in a place nicknamed the Trench. Each one's role was designated by terms like "FLIGHT," "CONTROL," "FIDO," "TELMU," and "GUIDO." Flight dynamics officers, guidance and navigators imagined themselves as pilots on the spacecraft, in an effort to be so involved in their responsibilities that they literally connected with each phase of the mission.[71]

However, none of them realized that the *Eagle* would overshoot its landing target, because they were too wrapped up in another dilemma: Mission Control had lost radio contact with the *Eagle*. The controls then made a succession of confirmations, whether the *Eagle* could continue its powered descent and land, or whether or not to abort the mission. Given the choice of "Go/No Go," the responses were unanimous. A solution to the problem had lay with using Collins in the CSM to relay Mission Control telemetry to the LEM. The mission could continue. The flight controllers were all "Go." Collins relayed the message to the *Eagle*, "*Eagle, Columbia*. They just gave you a go for powered descent...*Eagle*, do you read *Columbia*?" Aldrin sent back the response, "We read you."[72]

Aldrin called off the instrument readings for Armstrong to pilot the craft, who by this time already realized they would overshoot the target area by almost four miles. MOCR realized the issue too as the *Eagle* sped over the surface of the Moon much faster than anticipated. MOCR considered aborting but waved it off. The controller responded with "GOs", and MOCR then lost contact with the LEM again.[73]

Making matters worse, computer alarms began to sound off. First came "Error 1202." MOCR learned of the programming error, knowing a computer malfunction would stop the mission, and both Apollo astronauts and flight controllers had trained for these alarms. In simulations, they

[70] *Rocket Men*, 236.
[71] *Rocket Men*, 240.
[72] *Rocket Men*, 245-246
[73] *Rocket Men*, 247.

had faced every single imaginable situation that could go wrong with the computers, and what they had learned instructed them for their next decision: "Go/No Go". As MOCR conferred with each other, Aldrin and Armstrong continued to descend rapidly to the Moon's surface.[74] Aldrin would later state, "During the descent, when were started having problems with the computer, my attention was focused entirely inside the cockpit looking at the displays and trying to relay the information on the computer and also on the altitude and altitude rate meters to Neil so he could use this with his out-the-window determination as to where we should go to find a suitable landing place. Things were happening fairly fast and it was just a question of making sure the most correct thing was done from my standpoint at that instance. Not much time was allowed for reflection on the situation."[75]

Then another error alarm sounded, "1201." Guidance and Navigation in MOCR reflected on the simulations training sessions for what seemed to Armstrong to be an unbearable amount of time. He asked for a reading, concerned that the powered descent could not continue. Armstrong later explained, "The concern here was not with the landing area we were going into, but, rather, whether we could continue at all. Consequently, our attention was directed toward clearing the program alarms, keeping the machine flying, and assuring ourselves that control was adequate to continue without requiring an abort. Most of the attention was directed inside the cockpit during this time period and, in my view, this would account for our inability to study the landing site and final landing location during the final descent. It wasn't until we got below two thousand feet that we were actually able to look out and view the landing area."

After 15 minutes of deciding, MOCR finally concluded that the computer alarm signaled the computer's difficulty with complex commands. The guidance system was being flooded by too many commands, and MOCR reassured *Eagle* that it could continue the descent. Armstrong still had control, and MOCR gave him another round of "GOs." Powered descent continued.

Armstrong tilted the *Eagle* into the feet-first position to land and immediately realized the terrain did not offer a place to safely land. They flew over a crater field with boulders, some the size of cars, so Armstrong continued to fly the *Eagle* horizontally. MOCR noticed his speed and the time; in every simulated landing, and by intended design, Armstrong should have landed the *Eagle* by now. Moreover, the craft was intended to land automatically. It had not, because Armstrong could not chance the site below him, so he continued to manually control the *Eagle* and skim over the top of the boulder field about 200 feet off the ground.

Armstrong had a number of other things to consider. A message light signaled a thruster shutdown, but he knew from the hundreds of flight simulations this was not the case, and because he knew that, he could continue to land. Fuel was a bigger concern. He now needed to rapidly lower the *Eagle* to the ground. At 65 feet, the LEM had 60 seconds of fuel left. With the

[74] "Apollo 11 Crew Makes Ready," http://www.hq.nasa.gov/pao/History/SP-4214/ch9-4.html#source23
[75] *Rocket Men*, 248.

rate of speed Armstrong had commanded the *Eagle* to move at, the craft entered the "dead-zone" quicker than MOCR liked. Even if Armstrong did decide to abort, the ascent stage would not lift them off in time to stop their descent to the surface. They would crash with fuel or without it.

These events happened without any explanation from Armstrong, so no one in the MOCR knew why he had decided to take manual control. He never said anything, and the flight controllers only heard Aldrin call off the feet and the percent of remaining fuel: "Four forward. Four forward. Drifting to the right a little...Twenty feet, down a half...Drifting forward just a little bit; that's good..."[76]

When Armstrong saw a clearing, he began to land, and the descent engines kicked up a cloud of dust. One of the *Eagle's* foot sensors had made contact. Armstrong heard Aldrin call "contact" and shut down the engines before relaying a famous message: "Houston, Tranquility Base here. The *Eagle* has landed."[77]

Small disconnects typified the momentous moment of triumph. A world celebrated, NASA

[76] *Rocket Men*, 258.
[77] *Rocket Men*, 259.

fretted, Aldrin turned to his religion, and Armstrong prepared to walk out onto an alien world. While people all over the world celebrated the *Eagle's* touchdown, MOCR had to make a decision: "Stay/No Stay." Another problem developed immediately upon landing when a frozen dollop of propellant blocked the descent stage engine and produced an increase in temperature. Engineers feared an explosion of the fuel vapors, but the problem solved itself, allowing Armstrong and Aldrin to resume their checklists. They would soon exit the *Eagle* and walk on the Moon's surface, but first, Aldrin took out his personal belongings and prepared to take Holy Communion.[78]

Walter Cronkite holding up the *New York Times* headline

Once the Eagle landed, the plan was to have Armstrong and Aldrin spend a few hours completely shutting down the lunar module and then get some sleep. But Aldrin and Armstrong were too excited to sleep. Armstrong prepared for several tasks before he would step out onto the Moon, and it took him and Aldrin far longer than expected -- 3 hours -- to suit up in spacesuits that would protect them. Armstrong also had to deploy the boom arm with another unique responsibility; the boom possessed a video camera to transmit the images of his first step onto the Moon. Armstrong, used to problems at this stage, also had to step a full three-and-a-half feet to the surface, but his landing was so gentle that the shock absorbers did not compress.[79]

---

[78] *Rocket Men*, 266.

[79] "Ten Things You Didn't Know about the Apollo 11 Moon Landing," http://www.popsci.com/military-aviation-amp-space/article/2009-06/40-years-later-ten-things-you-didnt-know-about-apollo-ii-moon-landing

The picture of Armstrong taken by the camera on the boom

Just before 11:00 p.m. Eastern Daylight Time, Armstrong began his exit out of the *Eagle* and onto the Moon's surface. As Armstrong was departing the *Eagle*, he activated the television camera, beginning a broadcast watched live by hundreds of millions of people. As he left his first footprint on the surface and described the dust, Armstrong then began to give his prepared statement, "That's one small step for a man, one giant leap for mankind."

Ever since, historians have debated whether Armstrong actually tripped over the statement, because the transmission sounded like he said, "That's one small step for man." The transmission quality of the video and audio was less than optimal, and some believe that a cut-out in sound produced what most people heard: "That's one small step for...man, one giant leap for mankind." Theories continue to abound about the omission of one "a" in the statement. Whether it was the transmission quality, nerves, or how a "central Ohioan" talks is a matter that might forever be unsettled. But the debate about the missing "a" demonstrated how many people on the Earth witnessed his first steps onto the Moon.[80]

---

[80] "One small step for 'a'...and a machine," http://www.collectspace.com/news/news-100306a.html; "Neil

Once he had made his first step, Armstrong let MOCR know what the surface was like, transmitting the message, "Yes, the surface is fine and powdery. I can kick it up loosely with my toe. It does adhere in fine layers, like powdered charcoal, to the sole and sides of my boots. I only go in a small fraction of an inch, maybe an eighth of an inch, but I can see the footprints of my boots and the treads in the fine, sandy particles." Armstrong would report that given the lack of gravity moving on the Moon was "even perhaps easier than the simulations...It's absolutely no trouble to walk around." Armstrong was so excited during his time on the Moon that his metabolic readings were worrying MOCR back on Earth, and they let him know about it.

Aldrin stepped out next onto the Moon, with a reminder from the MOCR to not lock the door, since the *Eagle* did not have a handle on the outside. Aldrin passed that test and made his own "small step for a man". He had now fulfilled his previous wish to join the "adventures" of the astronaut corps, going one step further onto another world, one he described for the ages as "magnificent desolation."[81] Aldrin later described the feeling:

"Well, the first thing that I wanted to do when I got on the surface was to hold on and to just sort of bounce around and check the mobility that I had and then let go and see what the footing was like. All that took was maybe 30 seconds or a minute to feel that I knew how to move around with great confidence, and that's all the later crews really needed to do. So I was doing that for my benefit but for their benefit too. And later on in the spacewalk outside, when I jumped around and pranced around, again I was doing that for the benefit of the people back on Earth to see, and to measure what the mobility was like, so that it would give something in addition to our verbal description of observations when we got back. The things that we did on that first mission I felt were done to make later missions more successful. So we would look and see what the condition of the lander was, take pictures of it, so that later on the people wouldn't have to spend the time doing that. Our mission really was to put out some simple experiments: the laser reflector, the passive seismometer, to verify that the leveling devices and the antennas worked, to do some quick sampling of the surface. Because our lander was heavier than the later landers, we didn't have the room for the consumables, or the margin, to be able to stay out to go twice, for example, or to stay out even longer. Whatever the flight plan, and the engineers decided what our mission was going to be, and how many hours we could stay out, that was it; there wasn't any point in saying 'Well, hey, let's change that so instead of staying out two and a half hours, we can stay out four hours.' Gee, the guys did the calculations and they said that's what you could do, so that's what we stuck with."[82]

Armstrong Didn't Misspeak on the Moon. That's How Ohioans Talk," http://io9.com/neil-armstrong-didnt-misspeak-on-the-moon-thats-how-510920446
[81] "Ten Things You Didn't Know About the Apollo 11 Moon Landing," http://www.popsci.com/military-aviation-amp-space/article/2009-06/40-years-later-ten-things-you-didnt-know-about-apollo-ii-moon-landing
[82] "Buzz Aldrin," To the Moon, http://www.pbs.org/wgbh/nova/tothemoon/aldrin.html

Aldrin's footprint on the Moon

Armstrong made sure to collect a Moon sample as soon as possible in case they had to quickly abort the mission and return to Collins and the *Columbia*. Now Aldrin focused on the two activities he had "crammed" the hardest for: the collection of geologically important samples and the use of a camera to document lunar surface exploration. In this he was successful, though with one twist. Aldrin only captured three photos of Armstrong on the surface of the Moon; and most of those photos did not show Armstrong straight-on. The reason for this omission lay with the time the astronauts spent on the Moon, two-and-a-half hours. They might have spent most of their time on the most difficult task of all: pounding the U.S. flag into the ground and unfurling it.[83]

[83] *Rocket Men*, 279; Apollo 11: Lunar Surface Journal, http://www.hq.nasa.gov/alsj/a11/a11.html; "Why It's So Hard to Find Photos of Neil Armstrong on the Moon," http://io9.com/5938190/why-its-so-hard-to-find-photos-of-neil-armstrong-on-the-moon ; "The Missing Man: There are No Good Pictures of Neil Armstrong on the Moon," http://www.theatlantic.com/technology/archive/2012/08/the-missing-man-there-are-no-good-pictures-of-neil-armstrong-on-the-moon/261622/

Armstrong's picture of Aldrin made sure to reflect the image of himself in Aldrin's visor

The astronauts also took seismic readings of the surface, collected several pounds of rocks and samples, and left a plaque and other memorials at the landing site. The plaque read, "Here men from the planet Earth first set foot upon the Moon, July 1969 A.D. We came in peace for all mankind."

Aldrin stands next to the Passive Seismic Experiment Package with the flag and the *Eagle* in the background

Chapter 16: Rendezvous

Armstrong and Aldrin entered the Ascent Stage with just enough time to take a phone call from President Richard M. Nixon, who told them:

"Hello Neil and Buzz, I am talking to you by telephone from the Oval Room at the White House, and this certainly has to be the most historic telephone call ever made from the White House.

I just can't tell you how proud we all are of what you have done. For every American this has to be the proudest day of our lives, and for people all over the world I am sure that they, too, join with Americans in recognizing what an immense feat this is.

Because of what you have done the heavens have become a part of man's world, and as you talk to us from the Sea of Tranquility, it inspires us to redouble our efforts to bring peace and tranquility to earth.

For one priceless moment in the whole history of man all the people on this earth are truly one—one in their pride in what you have done and one in our prayers that you will return safely to earth."

Still, one more problem remained that called for a solution: the arm switch on the ascent engine had broken off. With a ballpoint pen, Aldrin fixed the switch, and the Ascent Stage that engineers feared would not separate performed exactly as designed. The Eagle had "wings" again, and the astronauts rocketed into lunar orbit.[84]

While Armstrong and Aldrin had walked on the Moon, the *Columbia* had remained in orbit with Collins, the forgotten man in many ways. For every revolution he and *Columbia* made behind the far side of the Moon, he was truly the "loneliest man in the world." Ironically, he also belonged to another unique group of people as one of the only people to not witness Armstrong's first steps on the Moon. With a lot of time spent in solitude, Collins contemplated his surroundings and the influence of the experience. During every revolution, when he could finally see the Earth again, alone against the sea of black and stars, he pondered its position and state: "From space there is no hint of ruggedness to the [the Earth]: smooth as a billiard ball, it seem delicately poised on its circular journey around the Sun, and above all it seems fragile. Is the sea water clean enough to pour over your head, or is there a glaze of oil on its surface?...Is the riverbank a delight or an obscenity? The difference between a blue-and-white planet and a black-and-brown one is delicate indeed."[85]

As he stayed in orbit, he wrote, "I am alone now, truly alone, and absolutely isolated from any known life. I'm it...I feel this powerfully -- not as fear or loneliness -- but as awareness, anticipation, satisfaction, confidence, almost exultation. I like the feeling."[86]

That said, meditations and connecting with the universe should not suggest that Collins had nothing to do in orbit or nothing to worry about. At one point, a problem developed with the coolant system on the *Columbia*, a situation that put Collins on edge. He solved that problem, but

---

[84] *Rocket Men*, 281.
[85] *Rocket Men*, 275.
[86] *Rocket Men*, 289.

he still faced a bigger problem. The location of the *Eagle* on the Moon remained a mystery; and no one at NASA knew exactly where it had landed either. This could have meant trouble for the rendezvous between the two craft.

Picture of the *Eagle's* ascent stage heading toward *Columbia*

Since the Moon has no atmosphere, it was relatively easy for the *Eagle* to ascend without needing powerful rockets like the Saturn V. It only required the Ascent Stage with fuel propulsion engines to propel it back up to the *Columbia*, and once they linked back up, the ascent stage was jettisoned into orbit, eventually landing back on the Moon. The ascent was not without its issues either. One of the enduring images of the Apollo 11 mission was the planting of the American flag on the Moon's surface. Since the Moon has no atmosphere, there is no wind on the surface. Thus, the flag needed to be specially designed to remain completely unfurled. And with no wind on the surface, the intent was to have the flag stand forever. However, the mission's planners had overlooked one important detail. In one of the most unreported (and forgotten) aspects of the Apollo 11 mission, the ascent of the *Eagle* off the Moon's surface generated enough wind to inadvertently blow the flag over during liftoff. Aldrin watched the flag blow over and mentioned it during the ascent, making NASA aware of the issue. He later explained, "The ascent stage of the LM separated... I was concentrating on the computers, and Neil was studying the attitude indicator, but I looked up long enough to see the flag fall over." As a result, the astronauts on all subsequent Apollo missions made sure to plant the flag much farther away from the lunar module to avoid Apollo 11's mistake.

Collins could only look through the sextant and wait to sight the *Eagle*. He finally did, and after a complicated series of events to get the two ports to line up and hard dock, the latches clicked into place, and the *Eagle* and *Columbia* were reunited. The hatch was opened, and laughing and cheering began. Collins remembered the moment of reunion: "[I] grabbed Buzz by both ears and I was gonna kiss him on the forehead, I can remember that, and I got him to right about here and I said 'Eh, this is not a good thing to do somehow,' and I forgot, I clapped him on the back or shook his hand or something."[87]

Chapter 17: The Trip Home

The Moon's orbit is only a fraction of Earth's, so once the modules linked back up, the *Columbia* module was equipped with engines to propel it back toward Earth. The bigger concern for the return was that the modules had to reenter Earth's orbit at the proper angle to allow the planet to recapture it. Reentry into Earth's atmosphere subjects spacecrafts to temperatures of about 3,000 degrees Fahrenheit, so the module had an elaborate heat shield consisting of a mixture of dozens of panels, insulation and aluminum. A failure in any part of the heat shield system would be fatal.

As Apollo 11 made its way back to Earth, the astronauts broadcast one last time on July 23 and gave thanks to everyone involved. Collins told the audience, "The Saturn V rocket which put us in orbit is an incredibly complicated piece of machinery, every piece of which worked flawlessly ... We have always had confidence that this equipment will work properly. All this is possible only through the blood, sweat, and tears of a number of a people ...All you see is the three of us, but beneath the surface are thousands and thousands of others, and to all of those, I would like to say, 'Thank you very much.'"

Likewise, Aldrin told viewers, "This has been far more than three men on a mission to the Moon; more, still, than the efforts of a government and industry team; more, even, than the efforts of one nation. We feel that this stands as a symbol of the insatiable curiosity of all

---

[87] *Rocket Men*, 298.

mankind to explore the unknown ... Personally, in reflecting on the events of the past several days, a verse from Psalms comes to mind. 'When I consider the heavens, the work of Thy fingers, the Moon and the stars, which Thou hast ordained; What is man that Thou art mindful of him?'"

Armstrong said, ""The responsibility for this flight lies first with history and with the giants of science who have preceded this effort; next with the American people, who have, through their will, indicated their desire; next with four administrations and their Congresses, for implementing that will; and then, with the agency and industry teams that built our spacecraft, the Saturn, the Columbia, the Eagle, and the little EMU, the spacesuit and backpack that was our small spacecraft out on the lunar surface. We would like to give special thanks to all those Americans who built the spacecraft; who did the construction, design, the tests, and put their hearts and all their abilities into those craft. To those people tonight, we give a special thank you, and to all the other people that are listening and watching tonight, God bless you. Good night from Apollo 11."

Finally, it was time for the splashdown. The module had several "drogue parachutes," used for decelerating fast moving objects, which were used at about 25,000 feet. Those parachutes slowed the module down to about 125 miles per hour. Another set of parachutes would then slow the module down to about 20 miles per hour before it hit the water. Once the module splashed down, divers would deploy rafts to pick up the astronauts and anchor the module while a helicopter hovered overhead to collect everyone and everything. After being picked up, the returning astronauts would be quarantined for a period of time to study the effects the mission had on their bodies.

The splashdown of the *Columbia*

On July 24, Apollo 11 headed back to Earth and the splashdown in the Pacific Ocean, and the men would spend nearly a month in biological quarantine just to be careful. NASA had created an extensive but flawed process to protect the Earth from possible "Moon germs," but in the end the men would return home. Of course, their lives were never the same, and all three would leave NASA and the astronaut corps by the middle of the 1970s.

President Nixon visits the quarantined astronauts

Chapter 18: The Aftermath of Apollo 11

Apollo 11 may be the most famous space mission in history, but NASA only intended for it to be the first of many manned missions to the Moon. Within four months of Apollo 11's mission, Apollo 12 sat on the launch pad, ready to go to the Moon for a more extended duration. Apollo 12 is largely forgotten today, sandwiched between the two most famous Apollo missions, but it was actually one of the most successful Apollo missions. Although Apollo 11 was an obvious success, the mission encountered some problems, particularly the *Eagle's* descent to the Moon's surface. Apollo 12's mission was designed to correct the kinks, while also staying on the Moon longer to conduct more sophisticated experiments.

Apollo 12 landed on the Moon's surface using cutting edge Doppler radar, and almost all of the lunar module's descent was done automatically, both improvements over Apollo 11. Apollo 12 made a near perfect landing in the "Ocean of Storms," chosen because NASA knew its earlier unmanned probe, Surveyor 3, had landed there two years earlier. NASA wanted Apollo 12's crew to collect the probe's parts and bring them back for analysis. Apollo 12's crew also took more samples, tested the Moon's magnetic field, and set up instruments that would continue to transmit data to Earth long after the mission.

Apollo 13 likely would have faded into relative obscurity had it successfully completed its mission, because that has largely been Apollo 14's fate. Apollo 14 successfully analyzed the Fra Mauro highlands and crater by spending over 30 hours on the Moon's surface. Apollo 14 also debuted the "Modularized Equipment Transporter," a fancy name for what was essentially the Moon's first wheelbarrow. It allowed the astronauts to lug nearly 100 pounds of equipment and samples around on the surface. One of these astronauts was Alan Shepard, Jr., who a decade earlier had become the first American in space aboard Freedom 7.

Apollo 14 may have used the first vehicle on the Moon, but Apollo 15 trumped it on July 30, 1971, when it landed on the Moon with the Moon's first rover. Unbeknownst to the United States, the Soviets had put a tiny rover aboard Mars 3 and launched it toward Mars just two months earlier, but Apollo 15's Lunar Roving Vehicle was the first rover to land on another celestial body.

The Lunar Roving Vehicle became a staple of photographs and video shot during the final Apollo missions, and they are instantly recognizable today. The rover could travel about 10 miles per hour, allowing the crew to travel greater distances more easily in their bulky suits. Apollo 15's astronauts covered several miles on each rover, as did the astronauts of Apollo 16 and 17. All three rovers were left behind on the Moon's surface.

On the way back to Earth, Apollo 15 had the distinction of being the first mission to leave a satellite in Moon's orbit, allowing NASA to analyze the Moon's magnetic field, among other measurements. But Apollo 15 had been the fourth manned mission to land on the Moon in two years, and, at least to outside observers like President Nixon, each mission was accomplishing less noteworthy things. Except for the drama of Apollo 13, the missions never recaptured the original excitement of the first lunar landing mission, so it was only natural Apollo experienced a letdown. As the public's interest waned, missions were canceled, and the complete vision of the "Apollo Applications Project" would never be realized except for Skylab, the first and only American space station, which was fittingly launched by a Saturn V rocket.[88]

Less than a month after Apollo 15's mission, the Nixon Administration began pressuring NASA to pull the plug on the remaining Apollo missions. NASA had actually started doing the budget math nearly a year before Apollo 15 launched. In September 1970, NASA canceled two planned Apollo missions. But NASA was still able to launch Apollo 16 and Apollo 17 in 1972, with both missions placing an emphasis on the Moon's geology. Apollo 16 looked for volcanic

[88] *Rocket Men*, 30, 303; Google Moon, "Apollo Series," http://www.google.com/moon/; "Apollo 18: The Lost Apollo Missions," http://news.discovery.com/space/the-lost-apollo-missions-110902.htm;

activity among the Moon's highlands, while Apollo 17's crew included a professional geologist. On December 14, 1972, Apollo 17 Commander Eugene A. Cernan stepped off the Moon and back into the lunar module. No man has set foot on the Moon since.

Apollo 17 was the last Apollo mission. NASA ended up canceling three Apollo missions, designated today as Apollo 18, 19 and 20 even though two of those missions were to occur before Apollo 17. These missions were canceled due to budget cuts, and the materials for Apollo 20 were instead used for the Skylab, America's first space station.

By the end of the Apollo program, NASA had already begun designing and developing the Space Shuttle Program, which would provide reusable vehicles for manned space travel and theoretically save money.

A number of reasons explain why the U.S. succeeded and sent astronauts to the Moon. Each of the men who flew on those missions represented the best parts of the nation's efforts and willingness to make the sacrifice. The success may have been best described by the then-director of NASA, James E. Webb. He left office before Apollo 11's triumph, but his captured the essence of what made the Apollo program such a uniquely American success:

> "The nations of the world, seeking a basis for their own futures, continually pass judgment of our ability as a nation to make decisions, to concentrate effort, to manage vast and complex technological programs in our interest. It is not too much to say that in many ways the viability of representative government and of the free enterprise system in a period of revolutionary changes based on science and technology is being tested in space...[Society has] reached a point where its progress and even its survival increasingly depend upon our ability to organize the complex and do the unusual. We cannot do these things except through large aggregations of resources and power. [It is] revolution from above."[89]

Some have pointed out that the success of Apollo 11 and the program as a whole is made all the more remarkable by the fact that changes in society over time might preclude similar results. As one group of British scientists commemorating the 40th anniversary noted, "It was carried out in a technically brilliant way with risks taken... that would be inconceivable in the risk-averse world of today... The Apollo programme is arguably the greatest technical achievement of mankind to date... nothing since Apollo has come close [to] the excitement that was generated by those astronauts - Armstrong, Aldrin and the 10 others who followed them."

[89] *Rocket Men*, 177.

Picture of the *Columbia* at the Smithsonian National Air & Space Museum

Chapter 19: A Precision Lunar Landing

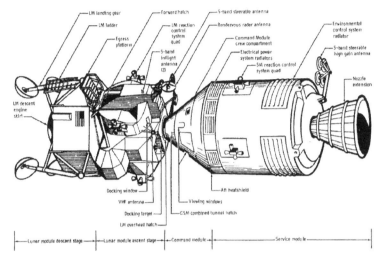

Apollo 13 space vehicle configuration.

A model of Apollo 13

"The Apollo 13 mission was planned as a precision lunar landing in the Fra Mauro highlands. The most significant changes to the planned mission profile from Apollo 12 were the maneuver to impact the depleted S-IVB stage on the lunar surface and the performance of descent orbit insertion using the service propulsion system. The S-IVB impact was intended to provide seismological data sensed by the instrument left on the moon during Apollo 12. Performance of the descent orbit insertion using the service propulsion system provides a greater propellant margin in the Lunar Module descent propulsion system, and this reserve would have been available during the critical precision landing phase." - NASA's *Apollo 13 Mission Report*

Superstition is a funny thing. Even the most scientific mind will rationalize not walking under a ladder for fear someone might spill the paint, or avoiding the path of a black cat since it might be sick or even rabid. Certainly the crewmen of Apollo 13 were intelligent, well educated men, and in fact, the three of them - Commander James Lovell, Jr., Command Module Pilot Ken Mattingly II and Lunar Module Pilot Fred Haise, Jr. - had worked together for years. As one newspaper article observed, the men "had trained together for two years and were described as a superbly conditioned unit." They were among the best and the brightest the country had to offer, part of an elite team that just about every young boy wanted to join.

According to NASA's biographical information on Lovell, he "was selected as an Astronaut by NASA in September 1962. He has since served as backup pilot for the Gemini 4 flight and backup Commander for the Gemini 9 flight, as well as backup Commander to Neil Armstrong for the Apollo 11 lunar landing mission. On December 4, 1965, he and Frank Borman were launched into space on the history-making Gemini 7 mission. The flight lasted 330 hours and 35 minutes and included the first rendezvous of two manned maneuverable spacecraft. The Gemini 12 mission, commanded by Lovell with Pilot Edwin Aldrin, began on November 11, 1966. This 4-day, 59-revolution flight brought the Gemini program to a successful close. Lovell served as Command Module Pilot and Navigator on the epic six-day journey of Apollo 8 - man's maiden voyage to the moon - December 21-27, 1968. Apollo 8 was the first manned spacecraft to be lifted into near-earth orbit by a 7-1/2 million pound thrust Saturn V launch vehicle; and Lovell and fellow crewmen, Frank Borman and William A. Anders, became the first humans to leave the Earth's gravitational influence."

Mattingly had nearly the same amount of experience, as did Haise. Of the latter, NASA said, "Haise was a research pilot at the NASA Flight Research Center at Edwards, California, before coming to Houston and the Lyndon B. Johnson Space Center; and from September 1959 to March 1963, he was a research pilot at the NASA Lewis Research Center in Cleveland, Ohio. ... He was the Aerospace Research Pilot School's outstanding graduate of Class 64A and served with the U.S. Air Force from October 1961 to August 1962 as a tactical fighter pilot and as chief of the 164th Standardization-Evaluation Flight of the 164th Tactical Fighter Squadron at Mansfield, Ohio. From March 1957 to September 1959, Haise was a fighter interceptor pilot with the 185th Fighter Interceptor Squadron in the Oklahoma Air National Guard. He also served as a tactics and all weather flight instructor in the U.S. Navy Advanced Training Command at NAAS Kingsville, Texas, and was assigned as a U. S. Marine Corps fighter pilot to VMF-533 and 114 at MCAS Cherry Point, North Carolina, from March 1954 to September 1956. ... Mr. Haise was one of the 19 astronauts selected by NASA in April 1966. He served as backup Lunar Module pilot for the Apollo 8 and 11 missions, and backup spacecraft commander for the Apollo 16 mission."

A picture of the original crew: Lovell, Mattingly, and Haise

However, in spite of their training and education, there was some talk about the possibility that the mission might be unlucky, or even cursed. Lovell later recalled, "I didn't even think about the number being superstitious. That is not true with my wife. My wife, Marilyn, said, 'Why 13?' ... It did bother me, yes. And I said, 'Well, what happened to 14?' ... I didn't feel invincible. I mean, the rewards involved overcame the risk that was involved."

Marilyn Lovell had other things to be worried about on the morning of the launch. She explained, "I was taking a shower and I'm—[my wedding ring] just slipped right off my hand and it went into the drain, and I just was terrified because, to me, it was like an omen that something really was going to happen. Oh, it did shake me up. ... For some reason or another the astronaut wives just never discussed anything that would worry their husbands before they went on a flight. I mean, we kept everything to ourselves."

Of course, the crew's boss, Gene Kranz, noted that the mission had to go on regardless of such things: "Superstition can't have any place. ... I think every person that was in this room lived to flaunt the odds. We were working on the ragged edge of all knowledge, all technology and all experience in this room." Kranz's home away from home was Mission Control in Houston, a place he once described as "having the smell of the cigarette smoke. …we all smoked very heavily, pipes, cigars, cigarettes, coffee pot that had been boiled over and had burned out. …whatever happened, we were better as a total team than the sum of the parts. … The work in this room is final. The decisions are final. The team in this room must be prepared not only to make those decisions, but to live with the results that occur."

Kranz

It should have been a routine mission, boring even, for Apollo 13 was not designed to do anything new or unique. In fact, it was supposed to more or less follow the path laid out for others. According to NASA's Mission Report, "The planned trajectory profile was similar to that for Apollo 12 except for descent orbit insertion being performed with the service propulsion system and the targeting of the spent S-IVB stage for a lunar impact. … The analysis of the trajectory from lift-off to spacecraft/S-IVB separation was based on launch vehicle onboard data…and from network tracking data. After separation, the actual trajectory information was determined from the best estimated trajectory generated from tracking and telemetry data. The earth and moon models used for the trajectory analysis are geometrically similar to those used for Apollo 12. … The planned launch and earth parking orbit phases for this mission were very similar to those for Apollo 12."

Nonetheless, the mission seemed plagued with bad luck from the beginning. First, there were problems with the training timeline, though in many ways these were nothing out of the ordinary.

According to one NASA report, "Crew training for Apollo 13 commenced on August 1, 1969. The crew was based in Houston until December 1, 1969, when operations were transferred to the launch site for final training. The training time was adequate to meet the planned launch date of April 11, 1970, and all training objectives were met. The only difficulty in coordinating the training activities was the scheduling of the lunar landing training vehicle for the Commander. The late availability of this vehicle, the large amount of time required for this type of training, and the need to travel between Houston and Cape Kennedy complicated the training schedule significantly. Because a primary objective was a field geology experiment as part of the second extravehicular excursion, considerable emphasis was placed on geology training. A week-long geology field trip to train the crew as "observers" was completed early in the training cycle. Later field trips emphasized practical geological procedures and timelines. Extensive use of field radios, extravehicular equipment, and assistance from mission control during these field trips made the training more effective."

Perhaps most notably, there was a crew change at nearly the last minute when Mattingly had to be replaced. NASA noted, "Several days prior to launch, the backup Lunar Module Pilot became sick with measles. Examinations of the prime crew indicated that the Command Module Pilot was not immune to the disease; therefore, the backup Command Module Pilot was substituted. The last 2 days prior to flight were devoted to integrated training among the three crew members, including the new Command Module Pilot. Flight results indicate that the last minute change of Command Module Pilots was practical and presented no training deficiencies, including readiness for the abort condition that occurred."

Thus, Mattingly was grounded and John L. Swigert, Jr. was sent in his place. Of him, NASA said, "Swigert held a position as engineering test pilot for North American Aviation, Inc., before joining NASA. He was also an engineering test pilot for Pratt and Whitney from 1957 to 1964. He served with the Air Force from 1953 to 1956 and, upon graduation from the Pilot Training Program and Gunnery School at Nellis Air Force Base, Nevada, was assigned as a fighter pilot in Japan and Korea. After completing his tour of active duty in the military services, he served as a jet fighter pilot with Massachusetts Air National Guard from September 1957 to March 1960 and as a member of the Connecticut Air National Guard from April 1960 to October 1965. He logged 7,200 hours flight-which includes more than 5,725 in jet aircraft. Mr. Swigert was one of the 19 astronauts selected by NASA in April 1966. He served as a member of the astronaut support crew for the Apollo 7 mission. Mr. Swigert was next assigned to the Apollo 13 backup crew and subsequently called upon to replace prime crewman Thomas K. Mattingly as Command Module pilot. (The substitution was announced 72 hours prior to launch of the mission following Mattingly's exposure to the German measles.)"

On the day of the launch, an Associated Press story reported about some of the blips that hampered Apollo 13 before it even left the ground: "The countdown for America's third moon-landing expedition proceeded because Swigert proved in a crash two-day trial that he could move from the Apollo 13 backup team to the first team. The decision to fly Swigert was made less than 24 hours before the scheduled launching. If Swigert hadn't made it, the launching would have been postponed until May 9 at a cost of at least $800,000. … Throughout the week, space agency officials considered postponing the mission, but decided to give Swigert a trial despite initial objections from mission commander Lovell, who wanted to keep his team intact. … But Lovell agreed, and Swigert slipped into a spaceship simulator with Lovell and Haise on Thursday to practice critical maneuvers that require split second timing by all three astronauts. The suspense built Friday morning when NASA Administrator Thomas O. Paine flew to Cape Kennedy to review the training and all other aspects of the flight. After 2 ½ hours, including a half-hour private meeting with Lovell, Paine gave the go-ahead to continue the mission with Swigert moving into the center couch of the Command Module as its pilot."

When asked about his meeting with Lovell, Paine later admitted, "Our first decision was that we would not let Mattingly fly. The rest of the meeting was devoted to the question of whether we could sub Swigert. … Jim was particularly disappointed that Mattingly couldn't make the trip. Jim has a high professional regard for him, and of course it was therefore very difficult for him to accept the decision he would not be able to fly with the…mission after all the many months of preparation that had put in."

Chapter 20: Midcourse Correction

"The space vehicle, with a crew of James A. Lovell, Commander; Fred W. Haise, Jr. , Lunar Module Pilot ; and John L. Swigert , Jr. , Command Module Pilot; was launched from Kennedy Space Center, Florida, at 2:13:00 p.m.e.s.t. (19:13:00 G.m.t.) April 11, 1970. … Prior to launch, a network of meters was installed in the vicinity of the launch site to measure electrical phenomena associated with Saturn V ascent in support of findings from the Apollo 12 lightning investigation; satisfactory data were obtained. During S-II stage boost, an automatic shutdown of the center engine occurred because of a divergent dynamic structural condition associated with that engine. Soon after the spacecraft was ejected, the S-IVB was maneuvered so as to impact on the lunar surface and provide seismological data. Following this maneuver, a series of earth photographs were taken for later use in determining wind profiles in the upper atmosphere. The first midcourse correction inserted the spacecraft into a non-free-return trajectory." - NASA's *Apollo 13 Mission Report*

In spite of its run of bad luck, once the Apollo 13 mission was finally in countdown mode, everything went off smoothly, with only minor problems. That morning, American newspapers proudly carried the following statistics:

"Astronauts: Navy Capt. James A. Lovell Jr., 42; civilian John L. Swigert Jr., 38; civilian Fred W. Haise Jr., 36.

"Purpose: Man's third moon landing. Lovell and Haise are to descend to the rugged highlands of Fra Mauro on the eastern edge of the Ocean of Storms where they hope to find rocks dating back perhaps five billion years to the creation of the moon. They are to deploy a nuclear-powered science station and drill 10 feet beneath the surface.

"Length of time on the moon: 33.2 hours, including 8-10 hours outside on the surface on two excursions.

"Names of space ships: Command ship, Odyssey; Lunar Module, Aquarius.

"Flight duration: 10 days, one hour, four minutes.

"Rocket: Three-stage Saturn 5, which with Apollo 13 spaceship stands 363 feet tall. The world's most powerful rocket, with a first stage thrust of 7.6 million pounds.

"Cost of mission: Saturn $185 million; command ship, $55 million; Lunar Module, $40 million; launch operations, including recovery operations, $70 million; scientific package, $25 million. Total $375 million."

It was the final point in the list that was beginning to divide the nation, as those vying for money from the federal government argued over whether it was appropriate to spend so much on more missions to the Moon when domestic programs instituted during the War on Poverty were struggling. After all, America had met its goal of landing a man on the Moon the previous year, so it became harder for NASA to justify continuing to go back.

Ultimately, NASA would have to scrap a few missions as a result of budget cuts during the early '70s, but in an attempt to stay in the nation's good graces and therefore keep its funding, NASA stepped up its public relations efforts and was working hard to portray its space program in the best possible light. As a result, the press was told a great deal about the purpose of Apollo 13's mission: to study the makeup of the moon's underground surfaces. As one article reported, "Two large pieces of Apollo 13 hardware are to crash on the moon to create massive manmade moonquakes which could tell much about the lunar interior. The 61-foot third stage of the Saturn 5 booster rocket is to smash with a force equal to 11 tons of TNT. The smaller Lunar Module – LM – cabin section, which will be impacted after the astronauts leave the moon is to hit with a force of 1.2 tons. The impact of the rocket stage, called an S4B, will be recorded by a seismometer left on the moon last November by the Apollo 12 astronauts. The Apollo 13 crew will plant a second seismometer, and they hope to crash their LM between the two instruments. When the Apollo 12 Lunar Module was crashed after it no longer was needed, scientists on the ground received a big surprise, as the seismometer recorded tremors for 55 minutes. On earth, a similar impact would reverberate only five or six minutes."

One geologist explained NASA's curiosity by saying of the previous moonquake, "This indicates that the structure beneath the surface of the moon is broken up, with a wide variety of fragments. The earth is solid and transmits a clear signal. If it weren't solid and the material beneath the surface were badly broken up, you would have many reflecting surfaces to distort the signal. That's the type of thing we saw with the Apollo 12 impact. But we don't know why it rang so long. The S4B is much larger and will give us a better energy calibration. We will get readings on the object with a known weight, speed and striking point."

There was another problem threatening the space program: the public was no longer as impressed by what they were doing. In spite of NASA's best attempts, there was little interest outside the scientific community in the moon's geology. As Lovell later conceded, "[Y]ou have to realize that human nature says that repetition means people get complacent, and people got complacent about Apollo 13. This was the third lunar-landing mission....It was just another day at the office." On another occasion, he commented, "As a matter of fact, before we took off I think the only mention of Apollo 13 in *The New York Times* was on the weather page about 97 pages in."

To be fair, it was not necessarily that rocket launches had become passé as much as it was that there were other, more pressing matters grabbing headlines, such as the war in Vietnam and the ongoing issues involving civil rights. Accompanying these issues was an increasingly anti-American sentiment among young people, a feeling that seemed to be spreading across the entire culture.

However, for those closely involved in the space program, a trip to the Moon was always a combination of thrills and a job to be done. As Haise put it, "Well, a liftoff, most people think...that would be a big kick in the pants. ...even though it has five engines running." Lovell also described what liftoff was like: "That's a long elevator ride up. Its 330-some feet. Just the crew, three of us, and a couple nervous checkout people are getting us into the spacecraft. ... Five and a half million pounds of high explosives in the form of oxygen, hydrogen and everything else. ...it's too late for jitters at that time. ...five, four, three... And those engines go, and you're on your way. ... That's when you have your hand close to the abort switch in case anything really goes wrong."

As one crewman working on Apollo 13 noted, the launch sequence mostly went well: "The prelaunch timeline was satisfactory, and adequate time was allotted for suiting and associated activities to meet the ingress time. The final count was smooth and communications with the Test Conductor and the Mission Control Center were adequate. After the fuel cell selector knob was rotated and had been in the new position for a short time, the fuel cell flow indicators would alternately rise several scale marks and then return to normal momentarily before cycling again. Since this effect was observed for all three fuel cells, the possibility of a sensor anomaly was dismissed. With the crew fully strapped down, some difficulty was encountered in removing the helmet protective covers just prior to egress of the closeout personnel."

Once the men were in place, all was set for "lighting her up." The countdown wound down as the engines fired up, and it was soon time for liftoff. However, not long after the launch was complete, the second stage inboard engine shut down suddenly, about two minutes earlier than it was supposed to. Fortunately, the crew was able to use the four outboard engines, along with the third-stage engine, to achieve the planned orbit 100 nautical miles above the earth's surface. Houston informed the crew that "we don't have too much of a handle on why the inboard cut off early except that it apparently was an engine problem and not a switch-select function. But we are certain that you'll be able to make TLI [trans-lunar injection] based on what we are looking at now." To that, Lovell replied, "Roger. There's nothing like an interesting launch." In hindsight, Lovell ironically remembered, "I looked at my companions, and I said, you know, every flight has a crisis. Something always goes wrong. This happened early in the flight, and we're now free and clear of any other things going wrong."

A picture of the launch of Apollo 13

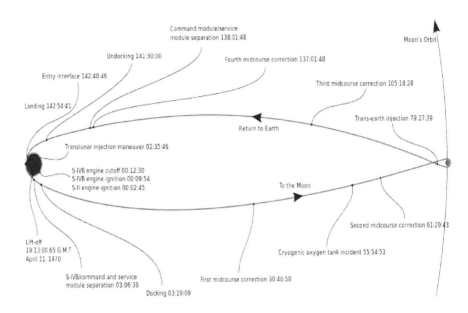

Command module/service module separation 138:01:48

Moon's Orbit

Undocking 141:30:00

Fourth midcourse correction 137:01:48

Entry interface 142:40:46

Third midcourse correction 105:18:28

Landing 142:54:41

Trans-earth injection 79:27:39

Return to Earth

Translunar injection maneuver 02:35:46

S-IVB engine cutoff 00:12:30
S-IVB engine ignition 00:09:54
S-II engine ignition 00:02:45

To the Moon

Second midcourse correction 61:29:43

Lift-off
19:13:00.65 G.M.T
April 11, 1970

Cryogenic oxygen tank incident 55:54:53

S-IVB/command and service module separation 03:06:39

First midcourse correction 30:40:50

Docking 03:19:09

The ultimate timing and trajectory of the mission, including a note of the incident and the necessary course corrections

Once the launch was over, the men aboard began working through their normal checklist of activities, beginning with the translunar injection, which consisted of a short thrust of power designed to get the ship pointed toward the Moon. Next, the crew had to "unpack" the Lunar Excursion Module from where it had been stored inside the upper stage, which required having to jettison that portion of the rocket, turn around and thrust their way back to the LEM in order to dock with it. Then they could send the stage toward its lunar destination. As one crewman commented, "Following separation and translation, a manual pitch maneuver of 1.5 deg/sec was executed. Computer control was re-selected, and a translation was initiated to give a small closing velocity. A digital autopilot maneuver was executed to align the respective roll attitudes. Maximum spacecraft separation was approximately 80 feet. At the final attitude, the image in the crewman optical alignment sight was almost completely washed out by the sun reflection from the Lunar Module until the vehicles were separated by 6 feet or less. Contact was made at approximately 0.2 ft/sec with a slight roll misalignment. Subsequent tunnel inspection revealed a roll index angle of minus 2.0 degrees. The handles on latches 1 and 4 were not locked and were recocked and released manually. Spacecraft ejection was normal. Total reaction control fuel used for transposition, docking, and extraction was reported as 55 pounds."

By the end of the second day, a sense of complacency had set in among everyone involved since things seemed to be going smoothly. The following exchange took place between Mission Control and the astronauts:

"Houston: Spacecraft is in real good shape as far as we're concerned, Jim. We're bored to tears down here. We do have a few little items for you, like a P37 update and a couple of flight plan updates. But there's no rush about them. Over.

Lovell: Okay. Gig us again in a few minutes. We're breaking out some food, and we'll copy them then.

Houston: Okay. And the surgeon will be ready for your sleep report whenever you get that together.

Lovell: Righto. If he's listening, LMP had a solid 9 hours of sleep; I couldn't wake him up this morning. The CMP had 6 hours, and the commander about 5 intermittent."

A picture of Mission Control shortly before the incident, with Kranz in the foreground

Chapter 21: An Immediate Abort of the Mission

"At approximately 56 hours, the pressure in cryogenic oxygen tank 2 began to rise at an abnormally high rate and, within about 100 seconds, the tank abruptly lost pressure. The pressure in tank 1 also dropped but at a rate sufficient to maintain fuel cell 2 in operation for approximately 2 more hours. The loss of oxygen and primary power in the Service Module required an immediate abort of the mission." - NASA's *Apollo 13 Mission Report*

A little over 50 hours into their mission, the astronauts took a break from their real work to do some public relations for NASA as part of a live broadcast from space. During the broadcast, the astronauts joked around for the amusement of the viewers back on Earth.

"Lovell: ...you've been looking at the—at Fred's workshop now, and you can see the abort guidance computer. And over there on the—tucked away in his armrest, is our activation checklist, which we'll be using very shortly. Up on the top of the window, we have our camera already mounted ready for photographing the descent. And now Fred's engaged in his favorite pastime, I found out on this flight so far.

Houston: He's not in the food locker, is he?

Lovell: That's his second favorite pastime. He's rigging his hammock for sleep on the lunar surface now to find out—to see what it's going to be like.

Houston: Roger. Sleeping and then eating.

Haise: It's kind of difficult here, Jack, getting into a hammock in zero g. I'm not sure if I keep floating away from it or it keeps moving away from me.

Lovell: If you notice a few things floating around, we found just about one or two washers occasionally.

Haise: And for the benefit of those that may wonder where Jim sleeps. Be a little difficult to rig his hammock in here right now with the hatch open, but his runs laterally in this direction, fore aft. So he has the upper berth and I get the lower berth."

There was just one problem with the broadcast: almost nobody was watching it. As Lovett explained, "One network had 'Dick Cavett' a live show. I think a second network had a rerun of 'Lucy.' And the third network, at least in the city of Houston, Texas, the baseball game was going on and everybody was watching that, including the people in the control center."

Ironically, NASA's greatest in-space disaster very nearly took place on live television, as it was only a few minutes after the astronauts ended their broadcast that disaster struck. At the end of the broadcast, Lovell moved through the ship to put away the camera they had used, and while he was doing that, Haise went to work to power down the Lunar Module. Meanwhile, Mission Control instructed Swigert to activate the stirring fans in the hydrogen and oxygen tanks in the Service Module to make sure their quantity readings remained accurate. According to Lovell, "It's sort of like a mush, this liquid oxygen, and so there's a fan down at the bottom of—inside the tank—it had a little heater system. And so the question was, 'Would you turn on the fan and the heater system and stir up the oxygen?' Merely flip the switch."

At that moment, something went terribly wrong. As Lovell later explained, "Haise had a reputation for being something of a prankster and for a minute he thought what he heard was just part of a joke. "It just had a big bang at one time, and so we all looked around, 'What happened? What's that?' I looked up at Fred Haise to see if he knew what was going on. ... And I could tell from his expression he had no idea." Haise added, "I'm sure he saw it in my eyes, and he saw I wasn't smiling. I heard the loud bang and metallic sounds because the way the vehicle contorted it actually twisted enough in the tunnel area that it crinkled the metal. You could hear that metal crinkling. ... And I knew it right away was not a normal circumstance." Then Swigert uttered the famous words, "OK, Houston, we've had a problem here," which Lovell repeated 15 seconds later. Kranz later admitted, "As soon as we received this call, it seemed our data just went wild. It was screwy. And for about 60 seconds it was literally chaos in this room. ... 'A flight, we've had a computer restart.' Another controller says, 'Main bus undervolt.' Third one says, 'antenna switch.' I immediately thought, 'OK, it's a minor electrical problem. We'll work this when the shift's over.' ... In the first few minutes there was absolute disbelief. The controllers had never come face to face with a real problem that we didn't have any immediate answers for."

Lovell later recalled, "One oxygen tank gauge, the quantity gauge, read zero. And the other one, I could see the needle start to go down ever so slightly and that's when I drifted over and kind of looked out the side window and I saw escaping, at a high rate of speed, a gaseous substance from the rear end of my spacecraft. ... And I realized the gas escaping and the needle on my second and last tank the quantity gauge, was one and the same, and shortly we'd be completely out of oxygen.' He told Houston, 'Looks to me, looking out the hatch, that we are venting something. We are—we are venting something out into the—into space. It's a gas of some sort.'"

In those desperate moments, Lovell described the sinking feeling the crew felt: "The low point was the explosion – which we didn't realize was an explosion until I saw the oxygen leaking outside the spacecraft, and saw from our instruments that we would be completely out of oxygen. This also meant we would be out of electrical power, and because we used the electrical power to control the rocket engine, we also lost the propulsion system. We knew we were losing the Command Module, but that was the only thing that had the heat shield to get us back to Earth."

He also admitted "the very first thing that I thought of, why didn't this happen on Apollo 12 or why didn't it wait for Apollo 14? ... The odds were very small at that time, among ourselves that we're going to get out of this alive."

While reading the data, the astronauts could only wonder what might have gone wrong. The most obvious answer was that the ship had been hit by a small meteoroid, and the crew would only later learn that when Swigert activated the switch to stir the tank, the circuits shorted out, setting fire to the insulation and causing the tank to explode. There may have also been a small, brief fire in the insulation lining the oxygen shelf compartment, and ultimately, one or both of these events popped the bolts off the 13-foot aluminum skin panel on part of the Service Module. Part of the panel hit the nearby S-band antenna and knocked out communication with NASA for almost 2 seconds.

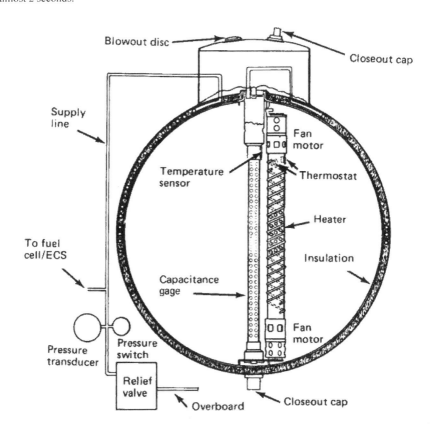

A diagram of the fuel tank

At the time, trying to figure out what happened would have to wait for later, because the crew now realized they would have to fight for their survival. The impact of the explosion had closed some valves that sent oxygen to two of the fuel cells, leaving them with only enough to operate for the next three minutes. The number 1 oxygen tank also ruptured and began leaking. After the mission, the pilot's report noted how unprecedented the incident was: "The trajectory had been very close to the nominal flight plan up to the time of abort, which was the first in the Apollo program. Throughout the manned space program, techniques have been developed and tested for the real-time determination of immediate abort requirements, but Apollo 13 presented the first situation in which their use was necessary."

Landing on the Moon was out of the question, and the astronauts immediately went about working their way through a list of emergency procedures, and as a result, they gave up on certain things in order to focus their attention on more pressing matters. The pilot's report explained, "Efforts to install the tunnel hatch were terminated when the Commander observed venting of material from the Service Module area. He then reported the oxygen tank 2 pressure was zero and oxygen tank 1 pressure was decreasing. This information pinpointed the problem source to within the command and Service Modules. At ground request, fuel cells 1 and 3 regulator pressures were read from the systems test meter, confirming the loss of these fuel cells. AC bus 2 was tied to inverter 1, and the emergency power-down procedure was initiated to reduce the current flow to 10 amperes. At ground request, fuel cell 1 and, shortly thereafter, fuel cell 3 were shutdown in an attempt to stop the decrease in oxygen tank 1 pressure."

In spite of the crisis, the men remained calm. As Kranz later pointed out, "This is why we flew experimental test pilots in the spacecraft. Their demeanor was such, when you listen to these reports and get the reporting that's coming in, they're just reporting a situation onboard the spacecraft. … We had an explosion with an enormous amount of corollary damage. … I think every controller at that time recognized, we're not going to the moon, but also it's going to be tough, damn tough, to get the crew of Apollo 13 home."

Meanwhile, Marilyn Lovell and her children had returned home from viewing the broadcast at Mission Control only to receive harrowing news: "And the phone rang. And he said, 'Marilyn, I just want you to know that all these different countries have offered to help, you know, in the recovery and whatever.' And I couldn't understand what he was talking about. And I said, 'Jerry,' I said, 'have you been drinking?' … And immediately [astronaut] Pete [Conrad] came out—and I can still see him standing across the room from me with eyes as large as saucers. And he said, 'Marilyn, we have to talk.' … I just couldn't believe what I was hearing, and at that moment the house was just filling with people. People didn't know what to say to me. Best friends, they couldn't say anything."

Chapter 22: The Abort Phase

"At the time of the incident, about 38 pounds of water was available in the potable water tank. During the abort phase, the crew used juice bags to transfer approximately 14 pounds of water from the Command Module to the Lunar Module for drinking and food preparation. The Command Module was completely powered down at 58 hours 40 minutes, at which time 99 ampere-hours remained in the three entry batteries. By charging the batteries with Lunar Module power, available battery capacity was increased to 118 ampere-hours. At landing, 29 ampere-hours of energy remained. Following Lunar Module power-up, oxygen, water, and battery power were consumed at the lowest practical rate to increase the duration of spacecraft support from a nominal 44 hours to a required 83 hours plus margins. In addition, the descent propulsion and reaction control systems were used to effect all required translation and attitude maneuvers following the incident." - NASA's *Apollo 13 Mission Report*

A picture of Apollo 13's Command Module

While their friends and family struggled with bubbling emotions, the astronauts and Mission Control remained calm, which was an absolute necessity when dealing with such an emergency. As Lovell put it, "From an emotional point of view…they didn't want to say to us, 'You have a real problem here.' And we didn't want to say to them, 'I think we got a real problem.' I mean, we knew that. ... How do we get out of this problem? What do we do? We don't know yet or just what the steps are to do that." Kranz added, "I was a fighter pilot. ... Fighter pilots from my time used the words 'looking into the eye of a tiger.' And this was the feeling I had when I recognized we were in survival mode and we had to kick in and get going as a team to help this crew out."

Knowing they were running out of oxygen in the Service Module, the men quickly decided to power it down so that they would still be able to use it for reentry later on. With that, they all moved into the Lunar Module, where they would remain until they figured out a solution. Lovell admitted, "Never thought I'd have to use that as a lifeboat. The Lunar Module was so fragile you could punch a hole through the skin in it. But we had to live off of it because it had oxygen. ... The only thing in the Command Module was a little battery and a little oxygen tank for the final plunge through the Earth's atmosphere. Jack Swigert was the Command Module pilot and I said, 'Jack, you power down this Command Module, save what you can. We're going into the Lunar Module, power it up...'"

The men knew that they had a lot of work to accomplish in a very short amount of time. Haise observed, "I knew the Command Module had only so much life left, and we very quickly had to get to a point in the startup of the Lunar Module before the Command Module completely died."

One of the things that they had to do was to transfer all the information they would need from the Command Module's computer to the Lunar Module's computers, which they accomplished this in a surprisingly primitive way. Lovell explained, "Jack Swigert called me all the numbers, and I wrote them down and then we had a conversion table for the Lunar Module. And I did the arithmetic to get the new numbers. And then I called mission control. I said, 'Would you check my arithmetic for me, please, to make sure I'm not making a mistake?' ...I'm using all the assets I have, and that included the control center."

The pilot's report also detailed some of the steps the astronauts had to take in the Lunar Module: "Lunar Module power up was handled quite efficiently by identifying selected segments of an existing procedure, the 'Lunar Module Systems Activation Checklist.' However, the crew had to delete the very high frequency portion of the communications activation. This procedure also assumed suited operations, so the crew had to turn on suit flow valves and un-stow hoses to establish air flow. This extended power-up blended well with the preparation for the subsequent endcourse maneuver to enter a free return trajectory. A similar real-time update to the 2-hour activation section of the 'Lunar Module Contingency Checklist' was also quite adequate. Lunar Module activation was completed at the time fuel cell 2 reactant flow went to zero because of oxygen depletion. The command and Service Modules were then powered down completely according to a ground generated procedure. To form a starting baseline for subsequent procedures, each switch and circuit breaker in the Command Module was positioned according to ground instructions."

While all three astronauts could fit in the Lunar Module, it was only designed to have two astronauts descend to the Moon in it, and most crucially, the Lunar Module could not take them back to Earth, because only the Command Module had the type of heat shielding necessary to withstand reentry. Moreover, while the Lunar Module could keep them alive, it was incredibly uncomfortable, as Lovell knew all too well: "It was about the temperature of your refrigerator. We didn't eat much food. We—and the water was freezing and the food was getting frozen, too. … I found out that I could be in front of the instrument panel, put my fingers together, close my eyes and for about three minutes, be asleep, wake up refreshed. And so that's essentially the— actually the sleep that we got on the way home." Haise echoed those sentiments: "It got pretty miserable. We had got out of storage all our spare underwear so we had three sets of underwear on."

A picture of the Lunar Module taken later in the mission

One thing that the men knew from their survival training was that in addition to oxygen, they had to have water to survive. To this end, as one reported, "Potable water was obtained by periodically pressurizing the potable tank with surge-tank oxygen and withdrawing potable water until the pressures equalized. This method provided potable water for crew use until 24 hours prior to entry, at which time water could not be withdrawn from the potable tank and it appeared to be exhausted." Needless to say, by the time they splashed down, these men needed more than one kind of stiff drink.

Then there was the matter of where to put the items that had never been intended to remain in the ship. According to one of the crew, "The hatch, probe, and drogue were secured in the couches by lap belt and shoulder harness restraints to prevent movement during subsequent maneuvers."

Through it all, the men remained stoic, at least on the outside. According to Lovell, "To ourselves we thought about family not to each other…we did not bring that up. And we did not because we did not want to get emotionally disturbed or challenged from the job that we had to do." Conversely, things were quite different for their families, as Marilyn Lovell recalled: "Friends of mine told me that I was in a daze really. The house was packed. And I just had to be by myself. And I just left everyone. And I had gone into the bathroom and I kneeled on the tile floor and prayed."

Meanwhile, Kranz and his team were focused on how best to get the crew home: "I had a very fundamental decision I had to make. We could execute what we call a direct abort and come around the front side of the moon and be home in a day and a half. If this maneuver isn't executed perfectly, you're going to impact the moon. … The other option I—you'd have to go completely around the moon, take between four and five days to get back home. … And it was purely in a gut feeling that says go around the moon, take your chances, trust your team to find the answers."

Houston also had a few more survival suggestions, some of which made an already tense situation even more unpleasant. Command radioed the men, "We recommend for sleeping that you leave one guy on watch. We recommend you don't make any urine dumps if you can help it, because it'll make the debris problem worse than it is now. And we have some items that you might want to transfer to the LM, some towels, some penlights, fecal bags, UTS. And do you have any more items that we can help you out with at the moment?"

Even in the midst of their stress, the men could still appreciate the opportunity the chosen course provided them. Haise noted, "Well, it was obviously to me, great to have the opportunity to even just loop around the moon, but Jack and I did a lot of sightseeing as we went around the back side." On the other hand, Lovell had seen it before as part of Apollo 8 and wasn't as impressed, especially with the photography: "And I told them if they, you know, 'If we don't get back you're not going to get them developed.'"

A picture of the Moon taken by Apollo 13

Chapter 23: Executed with Sufficient Accuracy

"After powering up the Lunar Module, co-aligning the two platforms, and shutting down all command and Service Module systems following the tank anomaly, a maneuver was immediately performed to return the spacecraft to a free-return profile. The maneuver was performed as the second midcourse correction using the descent propulsion system in the docked configuration, a mode tested successfully during Apollo 9. The resultant landing at earth would have been at 152 hours in the Indian Ocean, with Lunar Module system intended to support the crew for the remaining 90 hours. Because consumables were extremely marginal in this emergency mode and because only minimal recovery support existed at this earth landing location, a transearth injection maneuver using the descent propulsion system was planned for execution 2 hours after passing pericynthion. Between these two maneuvers, an alignment check was made of the Lunar Module inertial platform to verify the maneuver would be executed with sufficient accuracy to permit a safe earth entry." - NASA's *Apollo 13 Mission Report*

Perhaps the most important problem the astronauts faced was getting their ship back on course since the explosion had altered its trajectory. They were able to accomplish this with a "descent propulsion system maneuver" about 6 hours after the incident, but they would have to make subsequent course corrections, and they would be using the Lunar Module to execute maneuvers it had never been designed or tested to do. According to the pilot's report, "The docked configuration was maneuvered manually to null out guidance system error needles using the thrust/translation controller assembly for roll and pitch control and the attitude controller assembly for yaw control. It was not difficult to control the docked configuration in this manner. There was, however, some concern as to the effect the use of the thrust/ translation controller assembly would have on the trajectory. ... There were no vehicle attitude excursions, and the firing time was as predicted. The abort guidance system was not powered up for this maneuver. After the free-return midcourse correction, the spacecraft was maneuvered manually to the passive thermal control mode attitudes. The passive thermal control mode techniques consisted of maneuvering in the pulse mode 90 degrees in yaw once each hour using the pulse mode."

While they were doing the maneuvers, conservation was constantly at the forefront of each man's mind given that they were far from home and had lost much of their supply of fuel and electricity. At the same time, however, there was no margin of error, and a midcourse correction that merely got close to the splashdown point instead of being right on it could actually mean crashing on land instead of dropping into water. When Lovell was subsequently asked if he ever doubted that they would make it back to Earth safely, his response listed some of the things that a failed midcourse correction could result in: "Well, naturally I think everybody does in a situation like this. Well, we didn't think about what the final results would be if we weren't successful. What would finally get to us? Running out of all kinds of electrical power? Getting on to an orbit that we couldn't correct? And being in an orbit around the Earth for hundreds of years."

As if all of that wasn't enough pressure on the astronauts, the pilot's report explained the difficulties involved in making these maneuvers manually from the Lunar Module: "Because the platform was not aligned with a passive thermal control mode reference matrix, yawing the vehicle each hour resulted in inner and middle gimbal angle deviations. The crew could not determine any standard procedure to keep the middle angle constant during the maneuver. As the spacecraft maneuvered from one quadrant to the next, the same thrust/translation controller assembly input would result in a different effect in controlling the middle gimbal angle."

Years later, Lovell would look back over what happened during the crew's final days in space and recall, "It was the most challenging flight of the space program. I think it is a monument to the ability of the people in the control center, the mission control team and the crew to take an almost certain catastrophe, losing all the electric power and oxygen and the propulsion system some 200,000 miles away from Earth and then successfully utilizing the Lunar Module to get home -- and solve each crisis as it came along. We turned each catastrophe into a successful recovery. That is the story on Apollo 13. We were as nervous as anyone in a difficult situation some 200,000 miles out trying to get home. It was a challenging flight, no doubt about it. The only experiment we completed on Apollo 13 was not on the original mission list. We didn't do it, the ground team took control of the third stage because we didn't need it any longer and released it. And it impacted the moon, of course through the impact, we learned a lot about the structure of the lunar surface."

Over time, one of the crew's deadliest enemies proved to be their own bodies. The Lunar Module was only designed to house two men for two days, so after housing three men for more than 24 hours, the device designed to filter out the carbon dioxide in their breath was taxed beyond its abilities. At that point, every breath each man took brought all three a little closer to death.

The good news was that the Command Module had extra filters, but the bad news was that they were square and therefore unable to fit into the round openings in the Lunar Module. This was the ultimate consequence of the Command Module and the Lunar Module being designed, engineered, and built by two different companies, but as Lovell pointed out, this was an understandable oversight that nearly proved fatal: "And, of course, it's a big engineering goof that we didn't have the same canister for both sides."

Eventually, Kranz and his team on the ground came up with the "mailbox" solution that would allow the men to convert the canisters to fit by using only the items in the Lunar Module with them. First, Houston gave them the list of items to gather: "two Command Module lithium hydroxide canisters, a roll of the gray tape, the two LCGs (liquid cooled garments), because we're going to use the bags from the LCGs, and one—one LM cue card—one of those cardboard cue cards which you will cut off about an inch and a half out from the ring. Now, I think that's all we'll need." Then came the instructions, which Lovell described: "Yeah, they said, 'Now take three feet of duct tape,' and we said, 'What? Three feet?' They said, 'Yeah, an arm's length of duct tape.'"

In fact, Mission Control nearly forgot to tell the astronauts about one other item that they'd need, but it came up while they were constructing the cartridge: "Okay, Jack. The next step is to stop up the bypass hole, which is the hole in the center of the bottom of the canister; we want to stop that up because we don't want to bypass the flow; and I forgot to tell you to get something to stick in that hole. We recommend that you either use a wetwipe, or cut off a piece of sock and stuff it in there, or you could probably even crumble up some tape and use that. Over."

A picture of Mission Control working on the "mailbox" solution

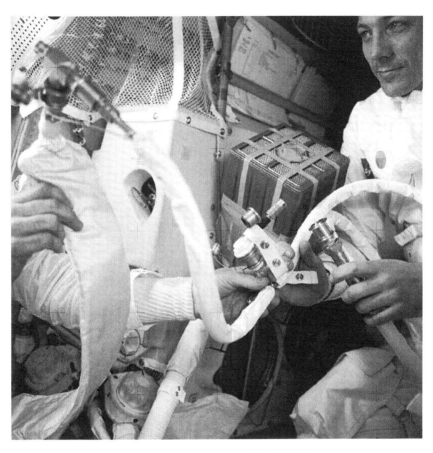

An onboard picture of the "mailbox" solution

While that problem was ultimately solved, there was another course correction needed. Lovell explained, "They call up and said, 'We've extrapolated your course all the way back to the Earth, and you're going to miss the atmosphere by...60 or 80 nautical miles, which meant, although they didn't say it, is that, 'Hey, you're gone.'" Thus, the men had to adjust their return trajectory without the aid of the computers they were accustomed to using, but by using Earth as a landmark, they executed the maneuver perfectly. According to Kranz, "Fred Haise was going, you know, to keep it from going sideways. And, of course, he's sick at this time and Jack is timing it because our clock had stopped, of course. ... This is the kind of relationship that we must have with our crew. The crew totally depends upon us to come up with the right answers.

We depend upon them to provide the information and to execute. So this…relationship is absolute, absolute. Trust is really the key."

Chapter 24: A Final Midcourse Correction

"The transearth injection maneuver was performed on time, and the transearth coast time was shortened such that landing was to occur at about 143 hours in the South Pacific, where primary recovery support was located. Guidance errors during this maneuver necessitated a small midcourse correction at about 105 hours to return the projected entry flight path angle to within specified limits. Following this firing, the spacecraft was maneuvered into a passive thermal control mode, and all Lunar Module systems were powered down except those absolutely required to support the crew. A final midcourse correction was performed 5 hours before entry to raise the entry flight-path angle slightly, and this maneuver was performed using the Lunar Module reaction control system under abort guidance control. The Service Module was separated 4-3/4 hours before entry, affording the crew an opportunity to observe and photograph the damaged bay 4 area. The Command Module was separated from the Service Module by using the Lunar Module reaction control system. The Lunar Module was retained for as long as possible." - NASA's *Apollo 13 Mission Report*

After speeding through space for four days, the time had finally come for the crew to leave their fragile lifeboat and return to the relative comfort and security of the Command Module. With only hours remaining until they were to reenter the Earth's atmosphere, the men began to slowly execute the steps necessary to get the Module up and running again, but in the back of their minds, they had to contend with the fact that no one had ever contemplated powering up the Command Module in space after four days without heat. In fact, some were not even sure it was possible.

As a result, the steps had to be figured out from the beginning, and ironically, it was left up to none other than Ken Mattingly, who had been grounded days before the launch. Once the incident occurred, Mattingly spent hours in the Command Module simulator to produce the exact sequence the astronauts were to use. Kranz subsequently admitted that Mission Control "went through four different versions of this checklist," while Lovell admitted, "I got a little testy and I said, 'Look it, give us the proper information, no more, no less.'" Even at this late juncture, there were small irritations. According to Haise, "We had no blank paper. So we had to rip covers and backs off of checklists and use that to write this checklist, which was very lengthy. … The Command Module did come fully up, you know, fully powered up. It was a ride home, ready or not."

According to NASA's report, "The unprecedented powered-down state of the Command Module required generation of several new procedures in preparation for entry. The Command Module was briefly powered up to assess the operation of critical systems using both onboard and telemetered instrumentation. Any required power in the Command Module had been supplied…from the Lunar Module through the umbilical connectors. It was through this means that the entry batteries were fully charged…. While these procedures represented a radical departure from normal operation, all were understandable and easily accomplished to achieve the desired system readiness. Equipment transfer and stowage in both the Command Module and Lunar Module was completed about 7 hours prior to entry, with the exception of the cameras that were to be used for Service Module photography. At 6-1/2 hours before entry, Command Module activity included powering up the instrumentation and placing entry battery C on main bus A, with main bus B still powered from the Lunar Module. The Command Module reaction control thrusters were preheated for 20 minutes, and all instrumented engines were observed to be above the minimum operating temperature 10 minutes after heater operation was terminated."

Next, it was time to make one more course adjustment, and again, they had to do it the old-fashioned way. "Lunar Module power-up for the final midcourse correction maneuver was performed according to the prescribed contingency checklist, with only minor deviations furnished by the ground. Shortly afterward, the Lunar Module windows cleared of moisture and the cabin temperature again became comfortable. Approximately 6 hours before entry, the passive thermal control mode was terminated and the spacecraft was maneuvered to place the earth in the crewmen optical alignment sight with the terminator parallel to the Y axis in preparation for the midcourse maneuver. At that time, a sun/moon alignment was made. Acquisition of these bodies was made by pitching up in a plane roughly parallel to the ecliptic plane. The sun filter made viewing through the telescope reticle very difficult. The spacecraft was controlled by the Lunar Module Pilot from commands given by the Commander, who responded when the reticle lines bisected the moon and solar disks. Three sets of marks were taken on each body. The initial maneuver to the firing attitude for the final midcourse correction was done manually using the earth as a reference in the same manner as the previous maneuver. This procedure presented no problems, even though the earth disk was considerably larger at this time. With primary guidance available, guidance system steering was manually followed to trim the spacecraft attitudes for the maneuver."

Once they were safely ensconced in the Command Module, the crew finally jettisoned the heavily damaged Service Module. NASA later reported, "Following the Lunar Module maneuver to the Service Module separation attitude, the Command Module platform heaters were activated, the Command Module reaction control system was pressurized, and each individual thruster was fired. … The Lunar Module was placed in an attitude hold mode using the abort guidance system…. The lightened spacecraft combination was easily maneuvered using attitude control in both the manual minimum-impulse and automatic attitude-hold modes."

It was then that the crew learned just how close they came to dying in space. In his description to Houston, Lovell observed, "There's one whole side of that spacecraft missing. … Right by the high gain antenna, the whole panel is blown out, almost from the base to the engine. … All right. She's drifting right down in front of our windows now, Houston. … And, Joe, looks like a lot of—a lot of debris is just hanging out the side near the S-band antenna." The report offered even further detail: "The Service Module first appeared in the docking window at a distance of about 80 feet. The entire bay 4 outer panel was missing, and torn Mylar insulation was seen protruding from the bay. Because of the brilliant reflections from the Mylar, it was difficult to see or photograph any details inside the bay. Initial photography of the Service Module was conducted through the docking window…. Upon completion of photography, the two docked vehicles were maneuvered back to the Service Module separation attitude in preparation for the Command Module alignment. Star observation through the Command Module optics in this attitude was poor because of light reflecting from the Lunar Module, and the Commander varied the pitch attitude by approximately 20 degrees in an attempt to improve star visibility. These attitude excursions, however, were not effective, and the spacecraft was returned to the original separation attitude for the Command Module alignment."

Pictures taken of the damaged Service Module later in the mission

Upon hearing how bad the damage was, some in Mission Control became concerned that the Command Module's heat shield might have been damaged. However, as Kranz later pointed out, "In our line of business, you only worry about those things that you can do something about." Lovell agreed: "That's right. There's nothing we could do about it. Never could go outside and repair it or anything like that. So we just—we just took it for granted that the heat shield was going to be intact."

As a result, there was nothing to do at that point but carry on. The Mission Report read, "At 2-1/2 hours prior to entry, the Command Module was fully powered up and Lunar Module power transfer was terminated. After Command Module computer activation, the unfavorable spacecraft attitude delayed communications signal lockup and the ensuing ground uplink commands. … Particles venting from the Command Module umbilical area impeded Command Module optics operation. With the Lunar Module attached to the Command Module and the Command Module optics pointed away from the sun, individual stars were barely visible through the optics."

With the Command Module approaching the time for reentry, it was time to bid farewell to their lifeboat. With nothing more it could do for them, the men jettisoned the Lunar Module with an affectionate, "Farewell, Aquarius. We thank you." NASA's report also described this process: "The maneuver to the undocking attitude was made by the Lunar Module. … Because of the difference in alignments between the two spacecraft, considerable difficulty was encountered in maneuvering to the Lunar Module undocking attitude…The maneuver required a complicated procedure using the Lunar Module platform and close cooperation between the Commander and Command Module Pilot. The resulting maneuver also used up considerable Lunar Module reaction control fuel. … Hatch closeout in both spacecraft was normal, and a successful Command Module hatch integrity check was made…The Command Module environmental control and autopilot systems were activated, and the Lunar Module was undocked 1 hour before entry. Lunar Module jettison was slightly louder than Service Module jettison and the Lunar Module was stable as it translated away using only tunnel pressure."

Chapter 25: The Fastest Recovery Time

"The Command Module was powered up with the three entry batteries, which had been brought up to nearly full charge using Lunar Module power. The Command Module platform was aligned to the Lunar Module platform, and the spacecraft were undocked 70 minutes before entry. After undocking, the escaping tunnel pressure provided the necessary separation velocity between the two spacecraft. From this point, the mission was completed nominally, as in previous flights, with the spacecraft landing approximately 1 mile from the target point. The Lunar Module, including the radioisotope thermoelectric fuel capsule used to power experiment equipment, entered the atmosphere and impacted in the open sea between Samoa and New Zealand at 25.5 degrees south latitude and 176 degrees west longitude, with surveillance aircraft in the area. The three crewmen were onboard the recovery ship, USS Iwo Jima, within 45 minutes of landing, the fastest recovery time for all Apollo manned flights."

In many ways, it was a marvel that Apollo 13 had come this far, but even at this point, everyone associated with the mission understood that in spite of their best efforts, there were still a number of things that no one could control. Lovell noted, "As we were going through and solving all the problems one by one, when we came back towards Earth and jettisoned the Service Module and saw the explosion had blown out the entire side panel, we wondered about that heat shield which was right behind us, if the explosion had cracked it. But there was nothing we could do at that point. There was no solution. You just crossed your fingers. Once we entered the atmosphere we just had to hope the heat shield was intact. And it was."

Back on Earth, Marilyn Lovell kept the faith, even in the face of overwhelming odds: "I really didn't give up. I just knew he'd be—come back." However, her daughter admitted how scared everyone was while waiting for the Command Module to approach Earth: "We all just sat there and we just held our breath. And we held it with the world." This was especially true during the four minute blackout when no one could reach the men in the tiny Command Module during reentry, a time period Kranz vividly described: "The crew is now on their own. There are no more give backs. … And there's no response. And we call again. It's now one minute since we should have heard from this crew. … Every controller in this room is standing staring at those clocks on the wall. One minute and 27 seconds after we should have heard from the crew, we get a ray of hope." When Swigert was able to answer at that point, Kranz recalled that "the emotional release in this room [was] so intense that literally every controller [was] standing, crying."

Having survived reentry, Lovell could gratefully describe Apollo 13's splashdown: "When that spacecraft splashed down and water came over the—over the windows, I said, 'Hey, we're home.' … It was just quiet, and we shook each other's hand…and we said, 'Hey, we made it again.'" Haise noted, "The capsule was still cold, even after entry. Smoky air, frosty air poured out of the hatch when the diver opened the hatch." Most importantly, as Kranz pointed out, "[T]his crew that had been living in a meat locker is finally out in the warm air of the South Pacific and they are home and they are alive."

A picture of Apollo 13's splashdown

A picture of Mission Control celebrating the splashdown

From the crew's point of view, the splashdown itself was pretty uneventful. The official report read, "The entry attitude and platform alignment were confirmed by a successful sextant star check and moon occulation within 1 second of the predicted time. The pre-entry check and initisization of the entry monitor system were normal. …the entry monitor system trace was unexpectedly narrow and required excessive concentration to read. The guided entry was normal in all respects and was characterized by smooth control inputs. … Landing decelerations were mild in comparison to Apollo 8, and the spacecraft remained in the stable flotation attitude after parachute release. Recovery proceeded rapidly and efficiently. Standard Navy life vests were passed to the crew by recovery personnel. For ease of donning and egress, these are preferable to the standard underarm flotation equipment. They would also quite effectively keep any unconscious crewman's head out of the water."

The men later learned just how many people around the world had been waiting for that moment when they emerged from their brush with death. NASA's final report on the subject noted, "The Department of Defense provided recovery support commensurate with mission planning for Apollo 13. Because of the emergency which resulted in premature termination of the mission, additional support was provided by the Department of Defense and offers of assistance were made by many foreign nations, including England, France, Greece, Spain, Germany, Uruguay, Brazil, Kenya, the Netherlands, Nationalist China, and the Soviet Union. As a result of this voluntary support, a total of 21 ships and 17 aircraft were available for supporting an Indian Ocean landing, and 51 ships and 21 aircraft for an Atlantic Ocean landing. In the Pacific Ocean, there were 13 ships and 17 aircraft known to be available over and above the forces designated for primary recovery support."

Of course, most of the support came from those trained to bring back their own: "Support for the primary recovery area consisted of the prime recovery ship, *USS Iwo Jima*, five helicopters from the Iwo Jima, and two HC-130H rescue aircraft. Later, the experimental mine sweeper, USS Granville Hall, and two HC-130H aircraft were added to the end-of-mission array. One of the helicopters, designated 'Recovery,' carried the flight surgeon, and was utilized for retrieval of the crew. Two of the helicopters, designated 'Swim 1' and 'Swim 2,' carried swimmers and the necessary recovery equipment. A fourth helicopter, designated 'Photo' was used as a photographic platform, and the fifth helicopter, designated 'Relay,' served as a communications relay aircraft. The four aircraft, designated O 'Samoa Rescue i, ___ 3._ and 4,' were positioned to track the Command Module after exit from blackout, as well as to provide pararescue capability had the Command Module landed uprange or downrange of the target point. The USS Granville Hall was positioned to provide support in the event that a constant-g (backup) entry had to be flown."

When splashdown finally came, it was a near textbook recovery operation, and after all its bad luck, Apollo 13 finally caught a break. The Mission Report noted, "The Iwo Jima's position was established accurately using a satellite navigation system. A navigation fix was obtained at 1814 G.m.t., April 17, 1970, and the position of the ship at spacecraft landing was dead-reckoned back to the time of landing and determined to be 21 degrees 34.7 minutes south latitude and 165 degrees 23.2 minutes west longitude. At landing a radar range of 8000 yards and a visual bearing of 158.9 degrees east of north (true heading) were obtained from which the Command Module landing point was determined to be 21 degrees 38 minutes 24 seconds south latitude and 165 degrees 21 minutes 42 seconds west longitude. This position is judged to be accurate to within 500 yards. The ship-based aircraft were deployed relative to the Iwo Jima and were on station 20 minutes prior to landing. They departed station to commence recovery activities upon receiving notice of visual contact with the descending Command Module."

Once the Command Module was in the water, it was up to the Navy to get the men the rest of the way home, and this part of the mission went off without a hitch. "The Command Module landed at 1807 G.m.t. and remained in the stable 1 flotation attitude. The flashing light was operating and the inflation of the uprighting system commenced about 10 minutes subsequent to landing. After confirming the integrity of the Command Module and the status of the crew, the Recovery helicopter crew attempted to recover the main parachutes with grappling hooks and flotation gear prior to their sinking. Swim 1 and Swim 2 helicopters arrived on scene and immediately proceeded with retrieval. Swim 2 deployed swimmers to provide flotation to the spacecraft, and Swim 1 deployed swimmers to retrieve the apex cover, which was located upwind of the spacecraft. The flight crew was onboard the recovery helicopter 7 minutes after they had egressed the Command Module, and they arrived aboard Iwo Jima at 1853 G.m.t. … One main parachute and the apex cover were retrieved by small boat and brought aboard. The flight crew remained aboard the Iwo Jima overnight and were flown to Pago Pago, Samoa, the following morning. A C-141 aircraft then took the crew to Hawaii, and following a ceremony and an overnight stay, they were returned to Houston. Upon arrival of the Iwo Jima in Hawaii, the Command Module was offloaded and taken to Hickam Air Force Base for deactivation. Two and one half days later, the Command Module was flown to the manufacturer's plant at Downey, California aboard a C-133 aircraft."

A picture of the crew aboard the USS *Iwo Jima*

The astronauts talking on the phone with President Nixon after the recovery operation

A picture of Lovell reading a newspaper article about Apollo 13's safe return

Obviously, an extensive investigation followed the joyful homecoming. In making its report, the investigating board observed, "The following findings, determinations, and recommendations are the product of about 7 weeks of concentrated review of the Apollo 13 accident by the Apollo 13 Review Board. They are based on that review, on the accident investigation by the Manned Spacecraft Center (MSC) and its contractors and on an extensive series of special tests and analyses performed by or for the Board and its Panels. Sufficient work has been done to identify and understand the nature of the malfunction and the direction which the corrective actions must take. All indications are that an electrically initiated fire in oxygen tank no. 2 in the Service Module (SM) was the cause of the accident. Accordingly, the Board has concentrated on this tank; on its design, manufacture, test, handling, checkout, use, failure mode, and eventual effects on the rest of the spacecraft. The accident is generally understood, and the most probable cause has been identified. However, at the time of this report, some details of the accident are not completely clear. Further tests and analyses, which will be carried out under the overall direction of MSC, will continue to generate new information relative to this accident."

As a result of the Apollo 13 incident, the Mission Review board made a number of recommendations for changes to the Apollo Lunar Module and LEM: "Significant modifications should be made to the SJI oxygen storage tanks and related equipment. The modified hardware should go through a rigorous requalification test program." The board went on to add, "This is the responsibility of the Apollo organization in the months ahead. In reaching its findings, determinations, and recommendations, it was necessary for the Board to review critically the equipment and the organizational elements responsible for it. It was found that the accident was not the result of a chance malfunction in a statistical sense, but rather resulted from an unusual combination of mistakes, coupled with a somewhat deficient and unforgiving design."

In its concluding remarks, the review board went out of its way to remind its readers that while there were obviously problems, the mission itself was a triumph. "In investigating the accident to Apollo 13, the Board has also attempted to identify those additional technical and management lessons which can be applied to help assure the success of future space flight missions...The Board recognizes that the contents of its report are largely of a critical nature. The report highlights in detail faults or deficiencies in equipment and procedures that the Board has identified. This is the nature of a review board report. It is important, however, to view the criticisms in this report in a broader contest. The Apollo spacecraft system is not without shortcomings, but it is the only system of its type ever built and successfully demonstrated. It has flown to the Moon five times and landed twice. The tank which failed, the design of which is criticized in this report, is one of a series which had thousands of hours of successful operation in space prior to Apollo 13. While the team of designers, engineers, and technicians that build and operate the Apollo spacecraft also has shortcomings, the accomplishments speak for themselves. By hardheaded self-criticism and continued dedication, this team can maintain this nation's preeminence in space."

As it turned out, none of the men who flew the Apollo 13 mission ever made it back to space. Having endured the terror that went along with what was ultimately her husband's final mission, Marilyn Lovell convinced Jim to remain on Earth, or at least within its atmosphere, for the remainder of his career. As a result, Lovell retired in 1973. Haise remained with NASA for another nine years, during which he helped develop and test the next generation of manned spacecraft: space shuttles. Tragically, Swigert left the dangerous world of space exploration only to die in 1982 of cancer, just weeks before he was to be sworn in as a United States Congressman.

Only Ken Mattingly, who never actually developed the measles that compelled NASA to preemptively ground him, went on to fly again. Mattingly made it to the Moon as the Command Module pilot for the Apollo 16 mission, and he later flew two space shuttle missions before retiring from NASA in 1985.

Chapter 26: The Final Apollo Missions

After Apollo 13, there were no Apollo missions for eight months, a lull about twice as long as the intervals between the previous missions, but ultimately, Apollo 13's close call did not deter NASA from continuing manned missions to the Moon. On January 31, 1971, Apollo 14 lifted off with the exact same mission Apollo 13 had.

Apollo 13 likely would have faded into relative obscurity had it successfully completed its mission, because that has largely been Apollo 14's fate. Apollo 14 successfully analyzed the Fra Mauro highlands and crater by spending over 30 hours on the Moon's surface. Apollo 14 also debuted the "Modularized Equipment Transporter," a fancy name for what was essentially the Moon's first wheelbarrow. It allowed the astronauts to lug nearly 100 pounds of equipment and samples around on the surface. One of these astronauts was Alan Shepard, Jr., who a decade earlier had become the first American in space aboard Freedom 7.

Shepard on the Moon during Apollo 14

The moment Apollo 14 is most remembered for is the "golf shot." Alan Shepard, Jr. and Edgar Mitchell had brought a modified "six iron" and a few golf balls on the mission. Shepard immediately had difficulty swinging the golf club in his space suit, which only allowed the astronaut to swing the golf club with one arm.

Shepard whiffed on his first few attempts, but he connected on his third and fourth attempts. Shepard lightheartedly claimed that the balls went several miles, a reference to the Moon's gravity being considerably less powerful than Earth's. The balls did not travel miles, but Shepard estimated that they did fly several hundred yards.

Apollo 14 may have used the first vehicle on the Moon, but Apollo 15 trumped it on July 30, 1971 when it landed on the Moon with the Moon's first rover. Unbeknownst to the United States, the Soviets had put a tiny rover aboard Mars 3 and launched it toward Mars just two months earlier, but Apollo 15's Lunar Roving Vehicle was the first rover to land on another celestial body.

The Lunar Roving Vehicle became a staple of photographs and video shot during the final Apollo missions, and they are instantly recognizable today. The rover could travel about 10 miles per hour, allowing the crew to travel greater distances more easily in their bulky suits. Apollo 15's astronauts covered several miles on each rover, as did the astronauts of Apollo 16 and 17. All three rovers were left behind on the Moon's surface.

A picture of the rover used during Apollo 15

On the way back to Earth, Apollo 15 had the distinction of being the first mission to leave a satellite in Moon's orbit, allowing NASA to analyze the Moon's magnetic field, among other measurements. But Apollo 15 had been the fourth manned mission to land on the Moon in two years, and, at least to outside observers like President Nixon, each mission was accomplishing less noteworthy things. Less than a month after Apollo 15's mission, the Nixon Administration began pressuring NASA to pull the plug on the remaining Apollo missions.

NASA had actually started doing the budget math nearly a year before Apollo 15 launched. In September 1970, NASA canceled two planned Apollo missions. But NASA was still able to launch Apollo 16 and Apollo 17 in 1972, with both missions placing an emphasis on the Moon's geology. Apollo 16 looked for volcanic activity among the Moon's highlands, while Apollo 17's crew included a professional geologist. On December 14, 1972, Apollo 17 Commander Eugene A. Cernan stepped off the Moon and back into the lunar module. No man has set foot on the Moon since.

Apollo 17 was the last Apollo mission. NASA ended up canceling three Apollo missions, designated today as Apollo 18, 19 and 20 even though two of those missions were to occur before Apollo 17. These missions were canceled due to budget cuts, and the materials for Apollo 20 were instead used for the Skylab, America's first space station.

By the end of the Apollo program, NASA had already begun designing and developing the Space Shuttle Program, which would provide reusable vehicles for manned space travel and theoretically save money.

The Apollo missions are celebrated for the historic firsts they accomplished, the dramatic return of Apollo 13, and the classic footage of moments like the planting of the Apollo 11 flag, the "golf shot," and the use of rovers. Lost amid all of this is the fact that the Apollo program was conceived to conduct important scientific research on the Moon, and much of what is known about the Moon came directly from the Apollo missions.

Astronauts collected hundreds of pounds of Moon rocks and surface samples during the Apollo missions. Two distinctly different types of rocks were found on the Moon: basaltic rocks and igneous rocks. In addition to having age differences of over three billion years, the basaltic rocks were mostly found in the Moon's mares (the darker regions seen from Earth), while the igneous rocks were found in the Moon's highlands (the lighter regions).

From these rocks, scientists have made several important findings, helping them develop a theory as to the Moon's creation. Analysis of the basaltic rocks indicated that there was past volcanic activity on the Moon as recently as 1.2 billion years ago. Moreover, some of the Moon's rocks were over four billion years old, nearly as old as the Earth itself. In addition to that, several Apollo missions conducted seismic readings of the Moon, which helped scientists determine the magnetic field and mass of the Moon. Beyond determining that the Moon's crust is thicker on the far side than on the near side, the Apollo missions also helped scientists determine that the Moon's core is probably still molten.

The research done by the Apollo programs has provided evidence in support of the most widely held theory for the Moon's creation: the "giant impact theory." According to this amazing theory, the young Earth was struck by another planetary body about the size of Mars over four billion years ago, and the impact created a debris field that eventually formed the Moon. The giant impact theory would explain the Moon's molten core, the age of some of the Moon's rocks, and the evidence collected by the Apollo missions that indicated there were once magma seas on the Moon's surface. Given the Moon's dry, barren surface, it is hard today to imagine that magma was once abundant on the surface, but the magma left "lava tubes," amazing formations in which a lava stream forms a crusty roof over the flowing lava underneath it. With the magma gone today, the lava tubes resemble caves.

In addition to being interesting, the Moon's lava tubes are natural locations for a base camp envisioned by the Bush Administration's space policy. The lava tubes would protect colonists and inhabitants from the Moon's wildly fluctuating temperature changes and the Sun's ultraviolet rays, both of which are more extreme on the Moon than on Earth due to the Moon's lack of an atmosphere.

After the Space Shuttle Columbia disaster in 2003, President Bush announced a new space exploration policy in 2004 as a bit of a rally cry, calling for the creation of a base camp on the Moon within the next 20 years. NASA began planning the Constellation Program, which would have renewed manned missions to the Moon around 2020. However, the Obama Administration recently reversed it, due in large measure to budget concerns. Obama canceled the Constellation program in the 2011 budget, leaving NASA's plans in flux. In addition, Obama's policy would save more money by having NASA depend entirely upon privately built spacecraft, essentially removing its decision making capacity for designing spacecrafts.

Although many people view this new space policy as a step backward, the cancellation of the Constellation program is also an acknowledgement that the Apollo program has already done an incredibly thorough job of exploring and researching the Moon. No man has exited Earth's orbit since the Apollo 17 mission, and that is not going to change for at least several more years.

Online Resources

Other books about the Space Race by Charles River Editors

Other books about Apollo on Amazon

Bibliography

Aldrin, Buzz (2005). Reaching for the Moon. Paintings by Wendell Minor (1st ed.). New York: HarperCollins. 40 pages. ISBN 0-06-055446-0.

Barbour, John Andrews (1969). Footprints on the Moon. Writers and editors of the Associated Press. Manuscript by John Barbour. New York. Associated Press. OCLC 26341.

Benson, Charles D.; Faherty, William Barnaby (1978). *Moonport: A History of Apollo Launch Facilities and Operations*. NASA History Series. NASA.

Cappellari, J.O. Jr. (May–June 1972). Where on the Moon? An Apollo Systems Engineering Problem. Bell System Technical Journal 51 (5). New York: American Telephone and Telegraph Company. pp. 955–1127. OCLC 17779623.

Floca, Brian (2009). Moonshot: The Flight of Apollo 11. New York: Atheneum Books for Young Readers. 48 pages. ISBN 978-1-4169-5046-2.

French, Francis; Burgess, Colin (2007). In the Shadow of the Moon: A Challenging Journey to Tranquility, 1965–1969. Outward Odyssey: A People's History of Spaceflight. Foreword by Walter Cunningham. Lincoln, Nebraska: University of Nebraska Press. ISBN 978-0-8032-1128-5.

Kranz, Eugene (2000). *Failure is Not an Option: Mission Control from Mercury to Apollo 13 and Beyond*.

Lattimer, Dick (1985). *All We Did Was Fly to the Moon*. Alachua, FL: Whispering Eagle Press.

Murray, Charles; Cox, Catherine Bly (1990). *Apollo: The Race to the Moon*. New York: Simon & Schuster.

Rahman, Tahir (2008). We Came in Peace for All Mankind: The Untold Story of the Apollo 11 Silicon Disc (1st ed.). Overland Park, Kansas: Leathers Publishing. ISBN 978-1-58597-441-2.

Thimmesh, Catherine (2006). Team Moon: How 400,000 People Landed Apollo 11 on the Moon. New York: Houghton Mifflin Company. 80 pages. ISBN 978-0-618-50757-3.Anderson, Clinton P. (1968), *Apollo 204 Accident: Report of the Committee on Aeronautical and Space Sciences, United States Senate, with Additional Views, Senate Report 956*, Washington, D.C.: U.S. Government Printing Office.

Made in the USA
Middletown, DE
31 July 2016